Hawai'i's Best Beaches

JOHN R. K. CLARK

# Hawai'i's Best
# Beaches

A Latitude 20 Book

University of Hawai'i Press, Honolulu

*For my family*
*Julie, Sachi, and Koji*

© 1999 University of Hawai'i Press
All rights reserved
Printed in Hong Kong

04 03 02 01 00 99   5 4 3 2 1

**Library of Congress Cataloging-in-Publication Data**
Clark, John R. K., 1946–
    Hawai'i's best beaches / John R.K. Clark.
        p.   cm.
    "A Latitude 20 book."
    Includes index.
    ISBN 0–8248–2116–5
    1. Hawaii—Guidebooks.   2. Beaches—Hawaii—Guidebooks.
I. Title.
DU622.C547      1999
919.690441—dc21                                    98–30326
                                                          CIP

Photographs by Nelson Makua.

University of Hawai'i Press books are printed on acid-free paper and
meet the guidelines for permanence and durability of the Council on
Library Resources.

Designed by Kenneth Miyamoto

*Kahakai, i ke kai hāwanawana ma ke one.*

The beach, where the sea whispers to the soul.

# Contents

# Contents

# Preface

During the eighteen year period from 1972 to 1990, I wrote a series of four books on Hawaiian beaches: *The Beaches of Oʻahu, The Beaches of Maui County* (including Maui, Molokaʻi, Lānaʻi, and Kahoʻolawe), *Beaches of the Big Island,* and *Beaches of Kauaʻi and Niʻihau.* Published by the University of Hawaiʻi Press, these books inventory every beach on all of the eight major Hawaiian Islands and provide physical descriptions, historical sketches, water safety information, and summaries of ocean recreation activities for each beach. Out of the 500 beaches that are identified in the series, I have selected fifty to be the subjects of *Hawaiʻi's Best Beaches.*

Selecting the best of anything is always a challenging project. All of us have our own opinions of what makes something the best in its class, and, of course, our opinions differ widely. To evaluate beaches, most of us devise some sort of informal rating system, and our rating criteria are based on features and activities that we like personally. We may want a beach that is close to home, safe for toddlers, sandy for sunbathing, rocky for fishing, or windy for windsurfing; and we may not care if it has any other features as long as it has that one special quality we desire. This may mean that the best beach for us is not necessarily the best beach for someone else. In spite of personal preferences, there are some common criteria that are used to identify a best beach. This is evident by beach attendance: the best beaches are usually the most popular, attracting the most people.

The rating system I used for *Hawaiʻi's Best Beaches* was developed by Dr. Stephen Leatherman, Director of the Laboratory for Coastal Research at Florida International University in Miami, Florida. An international authority on beaches, Leatherman produces an annual list of the best beaches in the United States and is the author of *America's Best Beaches*. The common criteria in his rating system are consolidated into four categories: physical environment, amenities, water safety conditions, and aesthetics. Physical environment includes air, water, and sand quality and the presence or absence of trash, noise, crowds, and crime. Amenities include the presence or absence of ocean recreation activities, facilities such as concessions, restrooms, showers, and parking, and public access. Water safety conditions include the presence or absence of lifeguards, rocks and reefs, high surf, strong currents, and dangerous marine life. And, finally, aesthetics include scenery, uniqueness of location, and the presence of wildlife such as sea birds, fish, turtles, or whales.

While I used all of Leatherman's common criteria to evaluate Hawai'i's beaches, there were four in particular that I required for a "best" beach. The first was the presence of sand. This sounds obvious, but many beaches are composed of less desirable particulate matter finer than sand, such as silt or clay, or materials coarser than sand such as pebbles, cobbles, and boulders. For most of us, however, sand is the most important physical feature for beaches. The sand, however, did not have to be calcareous, or "white," sand as long as the grains were sand-sized.

My second requirement was that each beach had to be a good swimming site, at least during periods of no surf. Swimming is the most popular ocean recreation activity in Hawai'i and in the rest of the United States, surpassing even fishing.

My third requirement was that each beach had to be accessible to the public by land, since most of us walk, hike, ride the bus, or drive to the beach. This requirement eliminated the beaches on Kaho'olawe and Ni'ihau, which are not accessible to the public by any means of transportation. As a matter of interest, there are beaches on both Kaho'olawe and Ni'ihau that would otherwise have made the list. The public access requirement also eliminated several of Hawai'i's best beaches that are surrounded by private property. Examples are Kīpū Kai and Donkey Beach on Kaua'i, and Kawela Bay on O'ahu, where a land development problem has deprived the public of its use since 1986.

Fourth, I gave special consideration to beaches that I believed to have unique physical features, natural resources, or recreational opportunities elevating them to "best" status even though they were lacking in other important rating criteria. Examples of these beaches are Green Sand Beach on the Big Island and Red Sand Beach on Maui, which are unique for their physical features not only among Hawaiian beaches but among all beaches in the world.

Most of Hawai'i's best beaches are also the most popular beaches in Hawai'i. They are the beaches that rank high in all the rating criteria, and they offer the attractions that most people are seeking when they go to the beach: clean, soft, white sand; clear water; restrooms and showers; lifeguards; and some exciting ocean activities. Each of the fifty beaches is described using a five-point key that includes its name, location, description, precautions, and highlights. The information in the keys explains what makes each beach special and why it is one of the best. I think you'll agree when you get there.

# Acknowledgments

My thanks to the following people for their valuable contributions: Nancy Brown, Mike Furukawa, Bill Gorst, Bruce Greenwood, Don Griffin, Alan Hong, David Kamaka, Ka'imi Mamuad, Chuck McCrary, Ted Meyers, Chris Mitsumura, Janet Renner, Lori Sablas, Bill Vogt, and Lynn Vogt.

And special thanks to my family and friends for their support and suggestions: Greg Ambrose, Paul Bartram, Koji Clark, Sachi Clark, Jason Clark, William Hamilton, Stephen Leatherman, Dwayna Logan, Kainoa Makua, Nelson Makua, Gayla Mowat, Alice Stanley, Audrey Sutherland, Julie Ushio, and Pat Young.

# Oʻahu

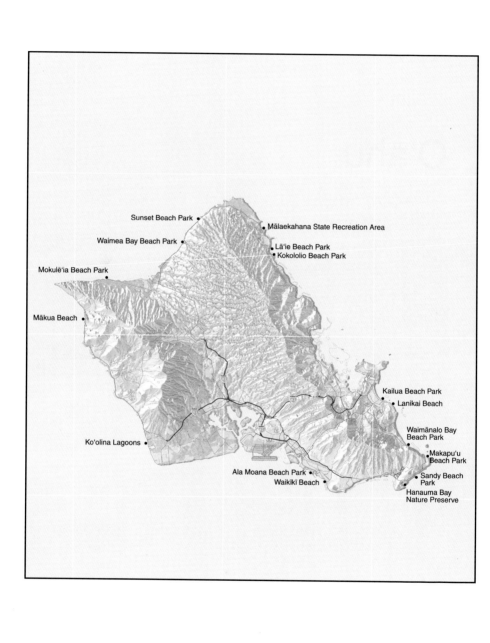

Sunset Beach Park •

• Mālaekahana State Recreation Area

Waimea Bay Beach Park •

• Lā'ie Beach Park
• Kokololio Beach Park

Mokulē'ia Beach Park •

Mākua Beach •

Kailua Beach Park •
• Lanikai Beach

Ko'olina Lagoons •

Waimānalo Bay
Beach Park •

• Makapu'u
Beach Park

Ala Moana Beach Park •
Waikīkī Beach •

• Sandy Beach
Park

Hanauma Bay
Nature Preserve

# Ala Moana Beach Park

**Location:** 1201 Ala Moana Boulevard, Honolulu.

**Activities:** Bodyboarding, fishing, scuba diving, swimming, surfing.

**Description:** Ala Moana Beach Park is the largest urban beach park in Honolulu and includes over 100 acres of picnic areas, softball fields, comfort stations, showers, food concessions, tennis courts, and parking. Fronting the park is a narrow white sand beach over one-half mile long with a deep swimming channel. The eastern portion of the park is a peninsula, extending seaward to a lagoon and a white sand beach, bordered by the Ala Wai Boat Harbor, the only boat harbor in Waikīkī.

**Precautions:** The Ala Moana Beach swimming channel is a former boat channel that was dredged out of the reef to depths of twenty-five feet. The ocean bottom in the channel drops quickly to overhead depths and water visibility is poor, so children and less experienced swimmers should stay near shore.

Swimmers should be aware that stinging box jellyfish *(Carybdea alata)* invade the swimming channel once a month. If you are susceptible to allergic reactions from bee and other insect stings, you should expect the same reactions from box jellyfish stings. Lifeguards are on duty daily. Check with them to find out if it is safe to swim. For more information on box jellyfish, see the Water Safety section.

**Highlights:** Ala Moana Beach Park is the most popular beach park in urban Honolulu. It is heavily used by swimmers, surfers, sunbathers, joggers, tennis players, model boat sailors, picnickers, fishermen, softball players, lawn bowlers, and strollers. Local families love beach parks, and Ala Moana offers one of the best combinations of park and beach activities in Hawai'i.

Prior to its development in the early 1930s, Ala Moana Beach Park was a tidal flat that served as the site of the city dump. In 1931 it was designated as Moana Park, and after several years of landscaping and construction, its facilities were completed. President Franklin D. Roosevelt, who happened to be passing through Honolulu, participated in the opening ceremonies during the summer of 1934. In 1947, the park's name was changed to *Ala Moana,* "path [to the] sea."

The deep channel fronting the park was dredged through the shallow coral reef during the late 1920s to connect the Ala Wai Small Boat Harbor and Kewalo Basin for boat traffic. As the popularity of the park increased, conflicts developed between swimmers and boaters, and eventually the City decided to close the channel to boaters. In 1955, a landfill project that is part of Kewalo Basin State Park closed the west end of the channel. In 1964, another landfill project, which is now popularly known as Magic Island, closed the east end of the channel and added approximately thirty acres of land to Ala Moana Beach Park. The security of the channel, closed at both ends and bordered on its seaward side by a wide expanse of shallow reef, makes it a popular, protected swimming site for families with children. It is one of the best beaches in Hawaiʻi for toddlers and older children who may be nonswimmers or inexperienced swimmers. Most families congregate near Magic Island, where the beach is widest and the parking is most plentiful. The length of the swimming channel (1,000 meters) makes it a popular training site for ocean swimmers and for swimming competitions. Several ocean swim events are held here annually, including swims that are parts of biathlons and triathlons.

The construction of Magic Island extended the park seaward across the reef right into the surf line, so the tip of Magic Island offers great photo opportunities of surfing and the Waikīkī shoreline. It is also the most popular spot in Honolulu to photograph Hawaiʻi's famous green flash, that brief but distinctive glow of green that appears over the sun the split second after it sets.

# Waikīkī Beach

**Location:** Waikīkī Beach fronts the entire Waikīkī resort area and extends from the Hilton Hawaiian Village to the Elks Club. It is accessible primarily from two streets, Kālia Road and Kalākaua Avenue, the main thoroughfare through Waikīkī.

**Activities:** Boat rides, bodyboarding, fishing, kayaking, outrigger canoe surfing, sailing, snorkeling, surfing, swimming, windsurfing.

**Description:** Although Waikīkī Beach is approximately two miles long, the "heart" of the beach fronts four hotels—the Sheraton Waikīkī, the Royal Hawaiian, the Outrigger Waikiki, and the

Sheraton Moana Surfrider Hotels—and Kūhiō Beach Park. This is where the highest concentration of sunbathers and swimmers is found, along with most of Waikīkī's beach concessions, and this is where Waikīkī's famous surfing waves are located. The concessionaires rent surfboards and bodyboards and offer surfing lessons and outrigger canoe and catamaran rides. Waikīkī Beach includes many individually named beach sections that primarily recognize the adjacent hotels or parks. From west to east these sections are Kahanamoku Beach fronting the Hilton Hawaiian Village Hotel, Kahanamoku Beach Park at the end of Paoa Place, Fort DeRussy Beach, the Outrigger Reef Hotel, Gray's Beach fronting the Halekulani Hotel, the Sheraton Waikiki Hotel, the Royal Hawaiian Hotel, the Outrigger Waikiki Hotel, the Sheraton Moana Surfrider Hotel, Kūhiō Beach Park, The Wall, Queen's Surf Beach, the War Memorial Natatorium, Sans Souci Beach, the Outrigger Canoe Club, and the Elks Club.

**Precautions:** During the summer months Waikīkī Beach experiences high surf at all of its surfing sites. Inexperienced swimmers and surfers should stay close to shore during these seasonal periods of high surf. Lifeguards are on duty daily. Check with them before going in the water. Fishermen should also be aware that the waters at Sans Souci Beach fronting the New Otani Kaimana Beach Hotel are periodically closed to fishing. Signs detailing the regulations are posted in the park.

**Highlights:** Waikīkī Beach is one of the most famous beaches in the world. Its warm waters and rolling surf have been attracting large numbers of visitors since 1901, when the first large tourist hotel, the Moana, opened for business. The Moana is still standing today (now named the Sheraton Moana Surfrider Hotel), and the Waikīkī resort area has grown around it to include approximately three square miles of hotels, condominiums, and shopping centers, bordered on the east by Diamond Head, on the north and west by the Ala Wai Canal, and on the south by Waikīkī Beach. While the resort area continues to evolve in its never-ending efforts to provide the optimum in accommodations, entertainment, recreation, and shopping opportunities, the beach remains constant with its offerings of warm sand, surf, and sun. And it is the beach that provides the foundation for the entire visitor experience.

One of the most famous attractions at Waikīkī Beach is its surf. Directly off the center of the beach are Queens and Canoes, the two surfing sites that have captivated visitors and residents since the early 1900s. Queens was named for Queen Lili'uokalani, the last reigning monarch of Hawai'i, whose beach home, Pualeilani, once stood in Kūhiō Beach Park, the park directly inshore from the surfing site. Canoes fronts the Sheraton Moana Surfrider Hotel, where its long, slow, rolling waves are the only waves in the world that are surfed daily by outrigger canoes. The waves at Canoes are also ideal for novice surfers.

Visitors tend to concentrate in the center and along the western end of Waikīkī Beach, but local residents prefer the eastern end of the beach fronting Kapi'olani Regional Park, where access is easy and parking is free. The Wall, the popular name for the drainage groin at the intersection of Kapahulu and Kalākaua Avenues, attracts bodyboarders from all over Honolulu, and to the east of The Wall, Sans Souci Beach fronting the New Otani Kaimana Beach Hotel offers a protected pocket of sand that is a family favorite for little children.

Waikīkī means "spouting water," a reference to the springs, ponds, and marshes that comprised much of the resort area prior to its development. In 1922, a major project was started to fill the Waikīkī wetlands and transform them into residential tracts. It was called the Waikīkī Reclamation Project and included dredging the Ala Wai Canal and pumping all of the dredged material, mostly coral, into the low-lying areas between the canal and the beach. This massive landfill project is the foundation of the resort area as we know it today.

# Hanauma Bay Nature Preserve

**Location:** 7455 Kalaniana'ole Highway, Hawai'i Kai. Part of Koko Head Regional Park.

**Activities:** Scuba diving, snorkeling, swimming.

**Description:** Hanauma Bay is a small, horseshoe-shaped bay located in Koko Head, a prominent headland at the southeastern end of O'ahu. Measuring approximately one-half mile from shore to its outer points and one-third mile from point to point, it contains a shallow fringing reef and a white sand beach approximately 2,000 feet long and 100 feet wide. Park facilities include restrooms, showers, picnic areas, snack bar, snorkel rental, tram service, park office, lost and found, and parking. The University of Hawai'i has an educational counter where staff members answer questions, hand out brochures, and conduct hourly walking tours at no charge. A fee is charged for parking and for entry to the beach. For park information, call 396–4229 (396–HBAY).

**Precautions:** Hanauma Bay is a marine life conservation district with strict regulations prohibiting all consumptive activities within its boundaries. Signs detailing the restrictions are conspicuously posted in the park, and park rangers can answer questions regarding the restrictions. Smoking is prohibited beyond the scenic lookouts.

During periods of high surf, powerful waves surge across the low lava terraces that lead out to the points on either side of the bay. When these conditions occur, the lifeguards close the gates across the terraces. Be careful walking on the terraces even when the gates are open, and pay special attention when you are crossing sections that are already wet from the wash of previous waves. Lifeguards are on duty daily. Check with them before proceeding beyond the beach if you are walking on the terraces or snorkeling beyond the reef.

**Highlights:** Hanauma Bay was created when the ocean breached the seaward side of a volcanic crater and flooded the crater floor. During the thousands of years that followed the breach, the erosive force of the ocean collapsed the seaward crater wall, and a massive reef and white sand beach formed at the head of the bay, creating one of the most popular snorkeling, scuba diving, and swimming sites in the world. The reef and the deeper waters in the outer bay are home to one of Hawai'i's most diverse and abundant populations of fish life.

In addition to offering snorkeling opportunities in a flooded volcano, Hanauma Bay is one of the most beautiful bays in Hawai'i, so the demand to visit, especially by the visitor industry, is very high. The demand, however, has had to be tempered with restraint to protect the bay's marine life and its environmental quality. The state took the first step in 1967 by designating the bay a marine life conservation district (MLCD) and terminating all consumptive activities. While the MLCD protected the marine life, during the next thirty years, negative impacts on the reef still continued as the visitor traffic escalated beyond the bay's carrying capacity. Finally, in 1990, the city initiated strict guidelines, including a limit of 2,000 visitors per day, to reduce the impacts of crowding so many people into such a small area. If your schedule permits, go early, before 8:00 a.m. during the summer months and the Christmas holidays and before 9:00 a.m. during the rest of the year. That should ensure that you will get in before the parking lot is full. Once the lot is full, security guards turn all cars away at the park entrance.

At the bottom of the beach access road, most beachgoers turn left, heading east. This is where the beach is widest for sunbathing and where the Keyhole, the largest pocket of sand in the reef, is located. The Keyhole attracts the majority of the swimmers and snorkelers in the bay. It was named for its shape, which resembles a keyhole when viewed from above. Beachgoers who are looking for less congested sunbathing and snorkeling opportunities should turn right and head toward the west end of the beach.

In December 1994, Hanauma Bay became the first "no smoking" beach in the United States. Cigarette butts, formerly the most profuse form of marine debris on the beach, have now almost completely disappeared, resulting in a less polluted and a smoke-free environment.

*Hanauma* means "curved bay."

# Sandy Beach Park

**Location:** 8800 Kalaniana'ole Highway, Hawai'i Kai.

**Activities:** Beachcombing, bodyboarding, bodysurfing, fishing, skimboarding, surfing, swimming.

**Description:** Sandy Beach is a wide white sand beach, approximately 1,200 feet long and 200 feet wide, that lies at the base of Koko Crater, which, at 1,208 feet, is the highest crater on the shoreline of O'ahu. Bordered on its west end by the famous Hālona Blowhole, Sandy Beach has a moderately steep, sloping foreshore and an ocean bottom that drops quickly to overhead depths. The quick change in depth creates steep, hard-breaking waves that form a pounding shorebreak. At the east end of the beach, waves also break on a rocky point and further offshore on an outer reef. Park facilities include restrooms, showers, picnic areas, a kite-flying area, and parking.

**Precautions:** Sandy Beach is subject to high surf at all times of the year. While this is one of its attractions, it is also one of its constant dangers, especially for those who dare to challenge its waves. The pounding shorebreak takes its toll every year in the form of dislocations, broken bones, and near-drownings. This is not a swimming beach unless the ocean is absolutely flat. It is normally a wave-riding beach for the experienced only. Lifeguards are on duty daily. Check with them before going in the water.

**Highlights:** Sandy Beach is one of the best shorebreak body-surfing and bodyboarding sites in Hawai'i, and its large, steep waves attract wave riders from all over the island. The surf breaks so close to shore that it affords excellent close-up viewing and picture taking opportunities. In addition, the steep foreshore at Sandy Beach provides one of Hawai'i's premier venues for skimboarding. Skimboard riders perform their spectacular sport by running after the trailing water of a receding wave with a small, thin board in hand. At just the right moment, they drop the board into the water, jump on it and surf across the sand at high speed, performing acrobatic manuevers as they go. If you have never seen bodysurfing, bodyboarding, or skimboarding in action, be sure to walk down to the water's edge for a spectacular show of athletic ability. And don't forget your camera.

During periods of extremely high surf, such as when hurricanes pass to the south of the islands, huge waves pour into Sandy Beach, severely eroding the foreshore and cutting sand banks up to six feet high. A beachcomber's delight, these nearly vertical cuts expose all of the loose change, rings, chains, and watches that have been jarred loose and lost during normal pounding surf sessions. When a "money swell" hits, dozens of treasure hunters brave the torrential winds and rains that come with the storm surf and scramble in the receding waves for anything that is exposed. No matter what the conditions, there is always something to do at Sandy Beach.

# Makapu'u Beach Park

**Location:** 41–095 Kalaniana'ole Highway, Waimānalo.

**Activities:** Bodyboarding, bodysurfing, fishing, swimming.

**Description:** Makapu'u Beach is located on the leeward side of Makapu'u Point, the easternmost point on O'ahu. A curved pocket of white sand approximately 1,000 feet long and 200 feet wide, the beach sits at the base of a sea cliff, bounded by lava points. During the summer months, when the ocean is usually calm, the beach is wide with a gentle slope, but during the winter months, it experiences a dramatic change in appearance. Seasonal high surf erodes the beach to half its width, exposing a large lava ledge at the water's edge.

**Precautions:** High surf at Makapu'u creates a pounding shore-break and swift inshore currents. The currents often run directly into the rocks in the center and at either end of the beach. High surf also generates powerful rip currents, including one that runs seaward at the north end of the beach and another that follows the sea cliff toward the lighthouse at Makapu'u Point. Lifeguards are on duty daily. Check with them before going in the water. Makapu'u is off-limits to surfers. The lifeguards can point out the extent of the restricted area.

**Highlights:** Makapu'u Beach is one of Hawai'i's most famous bodysurfing and bodyboarding beaches. Its popularity dates back to 1933, when the coastal road around the east end of the island was completed and people from all over O'ahu were able to drive there. On a high surf day, the waves at Makapu'u break in the middle of the bay off the center of the beach, providing long, exciting rides for bodysurfers and bodyboarders. Spectators, including visitors and residents, often fill the lookouts above the beach to watch the action below.

The vantage point of the lookouts above the beach also provides an excellent view of Waimānalo Bay and two islands immediately offshore. The smaller island is Kāohikaipu, commonly known as Black Rock. The larger island is Mānana, commonly known as Rabbit Island. Rabbit Island was for many years the home of a small colony of rabbits, but none of them remain today. Both islands are state seabird sanctuaries.

*Makapu'u,* meaning "bulging eyes," is said to have been a black stone with eight protrusions on it that resembled human eyes. Hawaiians regarded the stone as a *kino lau,* a physical manifestation of a supernatural person, in this case a woman called Makapu'u. The stone once sat on the point below the lighthouse but has not been seen there for many years.

# Waimānalo Bay Beach Park

**Location:** 41–043 Aloʻiloʻi Street, Waimānalo.

**Activities:** Beachcombing, bodyboarding, bodysurfing, fishing, surfing, swimming.

**Description:** Waimānalo Bay Beach Park is located in the center of Waimānalo Beach, one of the longest white sand beaches on Oʻahu. The entire beach is over three miles long, but the portion of it fronting the park is approximately three-quarters of a mile long. The beach is wide, and the ocean bottom slopes gently to overhead depths across a series of shallow sandbars. Small, one- to two-foot high trade wind-generated surf breaks on the sandbars all year round. Facilities in the seventy-five acre park include restrooms, showers, picnic tables, camping sites, and parking. Permits are required for camping. Lifeguards are on duty daily.

**Precautions:** The windward side of O'ahu, including all of Waimānalo Beach, is famous for its stinging jellyfish, the Portuguese man-of-war. If you are susceptible to allergic reactions from bee and other insect stings, you should expect the same reactions from man-of-war stings. Check with a lifeguard before going in the water to find out if it is a man-of-war day. If no lifeguard is on duty, look at the debris line on the beach and see if there are any man-of-war in it. If there are, you may want to reconsider going in the water. For more information on Portuguese man-of-war, see the Water Safety section.

At night, the single road into the park is chained, so if you are not camping and you plan to stay after sunset, be sure to note the park hours on the sign as you enter.

**Highlights:** Waimānalo Bay Beach Park is one of O'ahu's most popular family beach parks because of its close proximity to urban Honolulu and suburban Kailua and Kāne'ohe. The small, consistent shorebreak provides excellent bodysurfing and bodyboarding opportunities for children and other novice wave riders, and the park offers good sites for picnicking and camping among its many ironwood trees.

Many residents call this park Sherwood Forest, a name that predates the area's conversion to a beach park. Prior to its development, the park was a popular spot for stripping cars and other illegal activities, and the activities of the thieves that used the heavily wooded area were compared to those of Robin Hood and his Merry Men in England. *Waimānalo,* the Hawaiian name of the park, the beach, and the surrounding community, means "potable water."

# Lanikai Beach

**Location:** Along Mokulua Drive in Lanikai, Kailua.

**Activities:** Beachcombing, kayaking, outrigger canoe paddling, sailing, surfing, swimming, windsurfing.

**Description:** Lanikai Beach is a nearly straight white sand beach approximately one mile long with considerable variation in width. It narrows at both ends and widens in the middle. The south end of the beach has suffered severe erosion problems, threatening a number of homes. Home owners in this area have constructed seawalls or taken other remedial actions to protect their properties.

The ocean bottom slopes gently to overhead depths along the entire beach. This contour ordinarily would encourage small, trade wind-generated surf, but Lanikai Beach is usually surf-free. The wide fringing reef approximately one-half mile offshore functions like a breakwater, effectively diffusing most of the wave energy before it reaches the beach.

Two large islands, the Mokulua Islands, lie off the south end of the beach. They are popularly known as the "Mokes" or Twin Islands. The leeward shores of the islands have small beaches, a white sand beach on the larger island and a pebble beach on the smaller island.

**Precautions:** The Mokulua Islands are both state seabird sanctuaries that provide nesting sites primarily for wedge-tailed shearwaters. The shearwaters nest in burrows on the leeward faces of the islands. For their protection, access is permitted only on the beaches, and walking inland is prohibited. Signs detailing the restrictions are posted conspicuously on each island.

The Mokulua Islands are approximately three-quarters of a mile from the south end of Lanikai Beach. As inviting as they appear, they are a long upwind and upcurrent swim or surfboard paddle for novice swimmers and paddlers. Do not attempt the crossing if you are not experienced in the ocean. The islands are located seaward of Lanikai Reef, where they are subject to high surf, especially during the winter months. Be careful walking on the windward sides of both islands.

Six rights-of-way lead from Mokulua Drive to Lanikai Beach, but only three of them are public. The other three are for Lanikai residents and their guests. Be sure to read the signs on the rights-of-way and select one designated for public use. Other than the public rights-of-way, there are no beach park facilities in Lanikai. The nearest restrooms and showers are to the north at Kailua Beach Park. There are no lifeguards on Lanikai Beach.

**Highlights:** Lanikai is considered by many O'ahu residents to be the best swimming beach in Hawai'i. The water is clear and not clouded by stream runoff, the beach is clean, wide, and surf-free, and the setting is picturesque, with coconut palms lining the backshore and the Mokulua Islands off shore. For these reasons, Lanikai Beach attracts beachgoers from all over the island and is a popular location for commercial photographers.

The larger of the two Mokulua Islands is a popular destination for boaters, kayakers, surfers, and sailors, and its small beach is visited daily and especially on weekends and holidays. It is one of the few offshore islands in Hawai'i with a beach where people can land, swim, and picnic.

*Lanikai* means "heavenly sea," although to be correct Hawaiian, it should be *kailani,* with the adjective *lani,* "heavenly," following instead of preceding the noun *kai,* "sea." Lanikai, however, has been the name of this shoreline community since the first lots were offered for sale in 1926 and, subsequently, became the name of the adjacent beach. *Mokulua* means "two islands."

# Kailua Beach Park

**Location:** 450 Kawailoa Road, Kailua.

**Activities:** Beachcombing, boating, bodyboarding, bodysurfing, fishing, kayaking, outrigger canoe paddling, surfing, swimming, windsurfing.

**Description:** Kailua Beach Park is located at the south end of Kailua Beach, a crescent-shaped, white sand beach more than two miles long and from 50 to 150 feet wide. The portion of the beach fronting the park is approximately three-quarters of a mile long. The ocean bottom fronting the beach slopes gently to overhead depths across a series of shallow sandbars. Small, one- to two-foot-high trade wind-generated surf breaks on the sandbars year-round, primarily off the center and north end of the beach. Popoi'a Island, or Flat Island, as it is most commonly known, is a small, flat limestone island approximately one-quarter mile off the south end of the park. Surf breaks on a shallow reef on the south side of the island. Facilities in the park include restrooms, showers, picnic tables, a boat ramp, and parking. Lifeguards are on duty daily.

**Precautions:** The windward side of O'ahu, which includes all of Kailua Beach, is known for its stinging jellyfish, the Portuguese man-of-war. If you are susceptible to allergic reactions from bee and other insect stings, you should expect the same reactions from man-of-war stings. Check with a lifeguard before going in the water to find out if it is a man-of-war day. If no lifeguard is on duty, look at the debris line on the beach and see if there are any man-of-war in it. If there are, you may want to reconsider going in the water. For more information on Portuguese man-of-war, see the Water Safety section.

Popoi'a Island is a state seabird sanctuary that provides nesting sites primarily for wedge-tailed shearwaters. The shearwaters nest in burrows in the interior of the island. For their protection, access is permitted only on the perimeter, and walking inland is prohibited. A sign detailing the restrictions is posted conspicuously on the leeward side of the island.

**Highlights:** If you are a one-stop shopper for ocean recreation activities, Kailua Beach Park is the place for you. It has a long, beautiful beach where you can swim, surf, or sail. With the trade winds blowing year-round, Kailua is one of O'ahu's premier wind-surfing sites, and a number of shops in town offer rentals and lessons. Novice bodyboarders, bodysurfers, and surfers can always find a shorebreak wave to the north of the park. Bigger waves providing longer rides break alongside Popoi'a Island. These waves are surfed by just about everyone with a wave-riding craft: surfers, bodyboarders, ocean kayakers, surf skiers, one-person canoe paddlers, six-person canoe paddlers, twin-hulled boat sailors, and wind-surfers. Popoi'a Island is the "turn buoy" for the annual Popoi'a

Swim, a rough water swim that begins in the park, circles the island counterclockwise and returns to the park. The Waikīkī Swim Club holds the swim annually in June. Kailua Beach Park and Ka'elepulu Canal, the waterway that bisects the park, are heavily used for outrigger canoe paddling. Outrigger canoe regattas and twin-hulled sailing regattas are held at the park.

In addition to its water activities, Kailua Beach is one of the best beaches in Hawai'i for walkers and joggers. With sand that is fine and firmly compacted, the beach provides an excellent walking and jogging surface. Every July, the Mid-Pacific Road Runners Club uses the beach to put on the only organized beach run in Hawai'i. Runners start at the boat ramp and race to the north end of the beach and back. Running shoes are optional. The fine sand at the beach park also provides excellent material for sand sculptures. Every February, the School of Architecture at the University of Hawai'i at Mānoa sponsors a sand sculpture contest for its students fronting the main pavilion in the beach park.

*Kailua* means "two currents."

# Kokololio Beach Park

**Location:** 55–017 Kamehameha Highway, Hauʻula.

**Activities:** Bodyboarding, bodysurfing, fishing, surfing, swimming.

**Description:** Kokololio Beach is one of two nearly identical white sand beaches on the shore of Lāʻie Maloʻo Bay. The second beach is called Pounders. Kokololio Beach is approximately 2,000 feet long and 100 feet wide. Its foreshore is moderately steep, the result of high surf erosion throughout the year. Its backshore consists of low dunes, vegetated by large ironwood trees. The north side of the beach is backed by private beach homes, whereas the south side is backed by the beach park. Facilities include restrooms, showers, and parking.

**Precautions:** Kokololio Beach is exposed to the open ocean and high surf at all times of the year, but especially during the winter months. Wide fringing reefs border the sides of Lā'ie Malo'o Bay but do not block high surf from striking the beach. During the winter months, high surf generates a pounding shorebreak and strong rip currents. No lifeguards are stationed at this beach.

**Highlights:** Kokololio Beach is a long, beautiful crescent of white sand. Although it is located only 100 yards from Kamehameha Highway, it cannot be seen from the road because of the high, vegetated dunes. So, in spite of its proximity to the well-traveled highway, it is often deserted, except for fishermen and surfers. The beach is good for swimming when there is no surf. During periods of high surf, a surfing site called CYOs forms at the edge of the reef at the south end of the beach.

Kokololio Beach Park was once the private beach estate of the Castle family. Their beautiful two-story home was built on the dunes and surrounded by gardens filled with statuary. Area residents called the estate *Kākela,* Hawaiian for "castle," a name that is still used today. *Kokololio,* "gusty," is the name of a local wind that blows from the mountains to the ocean. *Pali Kilo I'a,* "fish watcher's cliff," is the limestone point in the center of Lā'ie Malo'o Bay that separates Kokololio and Pounders Beaches.

# Lā'ie Beach Park

**Location:** 55–205 Kamehameha Highway, Lā'ie.

**Activities:** Bodyboarding, bodysurfing, fishing, swimming.

**Description:** Pounders Beach at Lā'ie Beach Park is one of two nearly identical white sand beaches on the shore of Lā'ie Malo'o Bay. The second beach is Kokololio. Pounders Beach is approximately 2,000 feet long and 100 feet wide. It is fronted by a shallow sandbar that drops abruptly to overhead depths at the surf line. Its foreshore is moderately steep, the result of high surf erosion throughout the year. Its backshore consists of low dunes, vegetated by large ironwood trees. The north side of the beach is backed by private beach homes, whereas the south side is backed by the beach park. Koloa Stream terminates at the beach near the parking lot. In addition to the parking lot, facilities at Lāʻie Beach Park include only portable restrooms.

**Precautions:** Pounders Beach is exposed to the open ocean and high surf at all times of the year, but especially during the winter months. Wide fringing reefs border the sides of Lāʻie Maloʻo Bay but do not block high surf from striking the beach. During the winter months, high surf generates strong rip currents and a pounding shorebreak on the shallow sandbar. No lifeguards are stationed at this beach.

**Highlights:** Pounders Beach is a long, beautiful crescent of white sand that is one of Oʻahu's popular bodyboarding and bodysurfing beaches. It was named for its pounding shorebreak waves by the students of the Church College of Hawaiʻi in Lāʻie (founded in 1955 and renamed Brigham Young University–Hawaiʻi Campus in 1974), who established the beach as a popular social and recreational site.

Pounders Beach fronts Lāʻie Beach Park. Lāʻie, a Mormon community since 1864, is also the home of the Polynesian Cultural Center and the Mormon Temple. The town takes its name from a beautiful legendary princess named *Lāʻie* who is said to have been born and raised here. Her name means "ʻ*ie* leaf" and is an abbreviated form of two words, *lau,* "leaf," and ʻ*ie,* a woody, endemic vine *(Freycinetia arborea).* The ʻie vine was associated with royalty, and the saying *"Pua ka ʻie,"* literally the " ʻie vine blossoms," means "royalty is born."

# Mālaekahana State Recreation Area

**Location:** Kamehameha Highway, Mālaekahana.

**Activities:** Beachcombing, bodyboarding, bodysurfing, fishing, snorkeling, surfing, swimming.

**Description:** Mālaekahana Beach is a crescent-shaped white sand beach a little more than one mile long and varying in width from 100 to 200 feet. It curves between Kalanai Point to the south and Makahoa Point to the north and is backed by low dunes overgrown by ironwood trees. Most of the beach is fronted by a shallow sandbar, where the ocean bottom slopes gently to overhead depths.

Small surf generated by the trade winds usually breaks on the sandbar year-round.

A small, vegetated island is located off the north end of the beach at Kalanai Point. Its Hawaiian name is Mokuau'ia, but it is popularly known as Goat Island. A small white sand pocket beach forms the leeward shore of the island, which faces Mālaekahana Beach. This beach is protected from the prevailing winds and currents. A surfing site is located over a submerged reef off the windward side of the island.

Mālaekahana State Recreation Area is located at the south end of the beach at Kalanai Point. Park facilities include restrooms, showers, camping sites, and parking. A satellite section of the park called Mālaekahana State Recreation Area–Kahuku Section is located at the north end of the beach at Makahoa Point. Park facilities there include beach cabins for campers. No lifeguard service is provided at either park.

**Precautions:** Although Mālaekahana is not considered to be one of O'ahu's North Shore beaches, it is subject to the same high surf conditions experienced every winter on the North Shore. Although the surf here is not as high as farther north, it does generate strong longshore currents, especially in the narrow strait between Kalanai Point and Goat Island. This is an important safety consideration for anyone who is attempting to wade between the point and the island. On many occasions the currents have swept waders out of the shallows into the deeper waters of Lā'ie Bay, sometimes with tragic results. The best time to cross is when there is no surf and the tide is low. If conditions are not favorable, wait for another day. There are no lifeguards here. And if you do decide to make the crossing, wear *tabi* (Japanese-style rubber shoes) or running shoes. The ocean bottom is rocky.

**Highlights:** Mālaekahana is a long, beautiful beach that for many years has been a popular beach home site for residents of Honolulu. Although it is well known as an excellent beach for swimming and for beachcombing, especially for Japanese fishing floats ("glass balls"), it is probably best known for Goat Island, a twelve-acre limestone island covered with vegetation, primarily ironwood trees. Like almost all of Oʻahu's small offshore islands, Goat Island is a state seabird sanctuary, but permits are not required to visit as long as the birds are left alone. Wedge-tailed shearwaters use the center of the island for their nesting burrows, so this is an especially sensitive area during the summer months. Avoid stepping into a shearwater's burrow by limiting your explorations to the island's shoreline or to the single trail across it.

For most people, though, Goat Island's main attraction is not its birds but its beach. The island can be reached by wading across the narrow strait between the island and Kalanai Point, and its beautiful little cove of white sand is easy to find on the leeward side. The ocean bottom fronting the beach is shallow and sandy, an ideal place for children to swim. For many people, Goat Island is a special place that comes close to fulfilling the universal fantasy about being alone on a deserted Pacific island.

Mālaekahana is the name of a mythical person, the mother of Lāʻie. The legend of Lāʻie is mentioned in the Lāʻie Beach Park section.

# Sunset Beach Park

**Location:** 59–100 Kamehameha Highway, Sunset Beach.

**Activities:** Bodyboarding, surfing, swimming.

**Description:** Sunset Beach is approximately two miles long with a summer average width of over 200 feet, making it the widest white sand beach on Oʻahu. The portion of the beach fronting the beach park is approximately one mile long. During the winter months high surf erodes the beach and narrows it considerably. Park facilities include portable restrooms and roadside parking.

**Precautions:** High surf generates dangerous water conditions, including powerful shorebreaks, longshore currents, rip currents, and backwashes sweeping across the foreshore. The high surf season normally occurs during the winter and spring months, beginning in October and ending in May. Lifeguards are on duty daily. Check with them before going in the water.

**Highlights:** During the summer months, Sunset Beach is a popular roadside swimming stop for visitors circling the island, but its major attraction is its surfing waves during the winter months. Sunset Beach is one of the best surfing sites in the world, especially for big waves over ten feet high. It is the home of the Triple Crown of Surfing, one of the premier events on the professional surfing tour, and is the preferred site for many other surfing contests. Surfers the world over consider Sunset's waves to be among the most dangerous and challenging they have ever ridden.

Sunset Beach got its name during the 1920s when the first residential lots along the beach were marketed as the Sunset Tract. The tract was named for the spectacular sunsets that are seen so often from the beach.

# Waimea Bay Beach Park

**Location:** 61–031 Kamehameha Highway, Waimea.

**Activities:** Bodyboarding, bodysurfing, fishing, snorkeling, surfing, swimming.

**Description:** The shoreline of Waimea Bay is a broad white sand beach approximately 1,500 feet long and 150 feet wide. The width of the beach varies seasonally. Sand moves to the east end during the winter and to the west end during the summer. High surf during the winter months also erodes the foreshore and moves sand into the deeper waters offshore. This process reverses during the summer when the sand accretes, rebuilding the beach. The beach at Waimea is called a bay-mouth bar because its sand normally blocks the mouth of Waimea River. During periods of heavy rains, the river erodes the sand barrier and flows into the ocean, flooding the bay with murky brown water.

**Precautions:** High surf generates dangerous water conditions, including powerful shorebreaks, longshore currents, rip currents, and backwashes sweeping across the foreshore. The high surf season normally occurs during the winter and spring months, beginning in October and ending in May. Lifeguards are on duty daily. Check with them before going in the water.

**Highlights:** Waimea Bay is internationally famous as the home of some of the biggest surfing waves in the world. During the winter months, waves up to twenty-five feet high provide some of the most exciting and dangerous surfing conditions imaginable. When a big swell is running, surfers and spectators from all over the island crowd the shoreline of the bay to watch the action at the point. In addition, high surf produces a powerful, pounding shorebreak that itself may reach heights of ten feet or greater. The combination of the huge waves at the point and in the shorebreak generate some of the most dangerous nearshore currents and ocean conditions in Hawai'i. For this reason, Waimea has been the site of untold numbers of rescues, injuries, and fatalities. If you are not an expert big wave rider, stay out of the bay during periods of high surf. Come back during the summer when there is no surf and the water is as calm as a lake.

One of the most famous landmarks on the North Shore is the high tower on the northeast side of Waimea Bay. Originally, it was part of a rock crushing plant built by C. W. Winstedt in 1930. Winstedt had been awarded a contract to improve Kamehameha Highway from Waimea to Kahuku and had set up temporary quarry operations on the shoreline of the bay. He abandoned the site in 1932 after his project was completed. In 1953, the deteriorating quarry buildings were converted into a Catholic church, and the former gravel storage tower became the now famous church tower of the Saints Peter and Paul Church.

Another famous landmark in Waimea Bay is the Jumping Rock at the southwest end of the beach. On no surf days, especially during the summer months, adventurous swimmers climb to the top of this massive black lava rock and jump into the ocean twenty feet below. With such a short drop to the ocean, the height of the Jumping Rock is not so much the attraction as its status as the only jumping rock on the North Shore. For that reason, it is a social magnet for teens and young adults.

*Waimea* means "reddish water," like the color of the river after heavy rains.

# Mokulēʻia Beach Park

**Location:** 68–919 Farrington Highway, Waialua.

**Activities:** Beachcombing, bodyboarding, fishing, snorkeling, surfing, swimming, windsurfing.

**Description:** Mokulēʻia Beach comprises approximately six miles of narrow white sand beach approximately 150 feet wide between Kaiaka Bay and Camp Erdman. Mokulēʻia Beach Park is a twelve-acre park located midway along the beach. Park facilities include restrooms, showers, camping sites, and parking.

**Precautions:** High surf generates dangerous water conditions, including powerful shorebreaks, longshore currents, rip currents, and backwashes sweeping across the foreshore. The high surf season normally occurs during the winter and spring months, beginning in October and ending in May. There are no lifeguards anywhere along the beach.

**Highlights:** Mokulē'ia Beach borders some of the last undeveloped sections of shoreline on O'ahu. These sections are found primarily to the west of the beach park, and they attract beachgoers who want to get away from the North Shore surfing crowds or who are looking for a peaceful place to camp, fish, swim, or surf. Although high surf strikes this shore as hard as it does the beaches to the north of Hale'iwa, the extensive fringing reefs protect several nearshore sites and allow swimming and snorkeling even when the surf is up. One of the most popular of these sites is a large, shallow, sand-bottomed pocket in the reef off the west end of the Mokulē'ia Airfield. This area and others are also good for beachcombing. High surf and winter storms often deposit shells in the debris line, making Mokulē'ia Beach an excellent shelling site. Beachcombers are commonly seen walking the beach, scanning the debris line and sifting the sand for shells and other items of interest that have washed ashore.

Mokulē'ia Beach Park is the only developed public park west of Kaiaka Bay, and its facilities attract a variety of users, including runners, hikers, mountain bikers, and other non-ocean recreationalists. During periods of strong Kona, or westerly, winds, the park becomes a premier windsurfing site.

*Mokulē'ia* means "district [of] abundance."

# Mākua Beach

**Location:** Farrington Highway, Ka'ena Point State Park, Mākua.

**Activities:** Bodyboarding, fishing, swimming.

**Description:** Mākua Beach is a long wide white sand beach that curves for approximately one mile between two limestone points. The width of the beach is normally about 200 feet but varies seasonally because sand moves to the east end during the winter and to the west end during the summer. High surf, especially during the winter months, erodes the beach and moves sand into the deeper waters off shore. This process reverses during the summer when the sand accretes, rebuilding the beach. Like most of the beaches along the Wai'anae Coast, Mākua Beach is not protected by an offshore coral reef, so the foreshore remains steep throughout the year from its direct exposure to high surf.

**Precautions:** High surf generates dangerous water conditions, including powerful shorebreaks, longshore currents, rip currents, and backwashes sweeping across the steep foreshore. The high surf season occurs during the winter and spring months, usually beginning in October and ending in May. No lifeguards are stationed here, so if you are a first-time visitor and you are not sure whether it is safe to go in the water, ask a local resident. If no one else is around, find a safer swimming beach, such as the Ko'olina Lagoons, especially if there is high surf.

**Highlights:** Of all the beautiful beaches on the Wai'anae Coast, Mākua Beach is the most spectacular. Its long crescent of white sand fronts a deep, wide valley that is undeveloped and uninhabited. One of Mākua's greatest attractions is that it is the only coastal valley on O'ahu without housing or other development projects. Ironically, this is because the valley itself is a live firing range for the U.S. Army, known as the Mākua Military Reservation. Mākua Valley was inhabited until World War II, when it was taken over by the federal government for use as a live firing range. The use of the valley by the military since the early 1940s has kept it from being developed, but at the same time the danger from unexploded ordnance has left it unsuitable for any other use. For this reason, there is no public access to the valley inland of Farrington Highway. The only evidence of the former community is the graveyard of the Mākua Protestant Church at the east end of the beach. Today, Mākua Beach is part of Ka'ena Point State Park, an extensive shoreline park that includes the entire western tip of O'ahu.

*Mākua* means "parent," and the valley is identified in Hawaiian creation chants as the home of gods and demigods.

# Koʻolina Lagoons

**Location:** Between the Ihilani Resort and Spa, 92–1001 Olani Street, and the Barbers Point Deep Draft Harbor, Koʻolina.

**Activities:** Bodyboarding, fishing, snorkeling, surfing, swimming.

**Description:** The Koʻolina shoreline, a beachrock and limestone terrace that is the seaward edge of an elevated prehistoric coral reef, begins at Kahe Point Beach Park and ends approximately two miles south at the Barbers Point Deep Draft Harbor. Four large lagoons with white sand beaches approximately 1,000 feet long are located inland of the terrace between the Ihilani Resort and Spa and the harbor entrance. Small channels that cut through the terrace connect the lagoons to the open ocean. These channels allow water from the ocean to circulate through the lagoons, but at the same time they are narrow enough to prevent high surf from directly striking the beach. The ocean bottoms in the lagoons are sandy and slope gently to overhead depths. Swimming is safe, but the water clarity is normally too murky for snorkeling. The lagoons are identified by number, the First Lagoon being the one next to the Ihilani Resort and Spa and the Fourth Lagoon being the last one next to the harbor.

**Precautions:** The lagoons, including the beaches on them, are located inland of the certified public shoreline and are, therefore, the private property of the Ko'olina Resort. While public access to the lagoons is part of the development agreement, the activities within the lagoons are regulated by the resort. Signs posted along the shoreline walkway detail the activities that are permitted and those that are prohibited. Activities permitted within the lagoons include sunbathing, wading, swimming, and snorkeling. Body-boarding, fishing, kayaking, and surfing are permitted only seaward of the certified public shoreline. Lifeguards are on duty daily. Check with them if you need clarification of the regulations.

During periods of high surf, waves surge across the limestone terrace that fronts each of the lagoons. Be careful walking on the terrace and pay special attention when you are crossing sections that are already wet from the wash of previous waves. During periods of high surf, strong rip currents run out the channels that join the lagoons to the open ocean. Swimmers would be well advised to simply stay away from all of the channels at all times of the year.

**Highlights:** In the early 1990s, Hawai'i developer Herbert Horita cut four lagoons and a marina out of the Ko'olina shoreline during the initial construction phase of his resort and residential community. He then imported sand to create four artificial beaches, one in each lagoon. When the project was completed and the lagoons were opened to the public, the response was over-whelming, especially by families with children. The lagoons filled a real need not only for the visitors and residents of Koʻolina, but especially for the residents of the surrounding communities. There are no other nearby beaches that are protected year-round from high surf, and the lagoons are ideal for families with toddlers and other nonswimming children. With their beautiful landscaping, well-maintained facilities, lifeguard-protected beaches, and free parking, the Koʻolina Lagoons now are not only the most popular family beach areas in central Oʻahu, but are among the best beach destinations in Hawaiʻi.

*Koʻolina* means "to rejoice."

# Maui

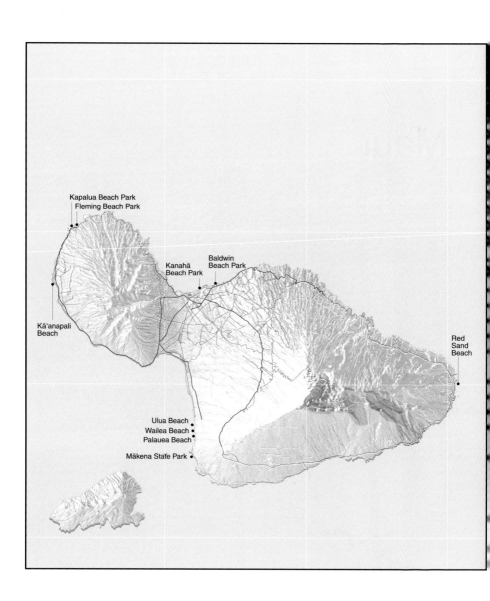

Kapalua Beach Park
Fleming Beach Park

Kanahā
Beach Park

Baldwin
Beach Park

Kāʻanapali
Beach

Red
Sand
Beach

Ulua Beach
Wailea Beach
Palauea Beach

Mākena State Park

# Kanahā Beach Park

**Location:** Alahao Road, Kahului.

**Activities:** Fishing, gathering seaweed, swimming, windsurfing.

**Description:** Kanahā Beach Park is a sixty-six-acre county beach park. The east half of the park is developed, with restrooms, showers, and paved parking. The west half is *kiawe* grove crossed by a number of secondary dirt roads. The beach fronting most of the park is narrow and severely eroded. A series of boulder groins constructed perpendicular to the beach to retard erosion have been ineffective and now are seaward of the beach and isolated in the ocean. However, a section of white sand beach approximately one-half mile long at the east end of the park is wide and free of rocks.

**Precautions:** Kanahā Beach Park is heavily used for windsurfing. Swimmers need to be alert at all times for windsurfers who are constantly launching and landing, often at high speeds. A swimming area near the east end of the park is delineated with a line of buoys to separate the swimmers and windsurfers. Kahului Airport is located directly inland of the park. If aircraft noise is too bothersome, you may want to look elsewhere for a more peaceful setting.

**Highlights:** Windsurfing was introduced to Hawai'i in the 1970s, and Kailua and Diamond Head Beaches on O'ahu immediately became its most popular sites. Then the sport moved to the north shore of Maui, where the shoreline from Kahului to Pā'ia has become one of the premier windsurfing sites in the world. The year-round consistency, high velocity, and angle-to-shore of the trade winds; the surf on the nearshore fringing reefs; the year-round mild climate; and the accessibility of sand beaches close to public roads have combined to make this a world-class venue for the sport and its international competitions.

Kanahā Beach Park, specifically the east end of the park, is one of the major windsurfing sites on Maui's north shore. On a windy day, an average of 100 windsurfers may be found in the water at any time of the day, and windsurfing boards and sails often cover the beach itself from end to end. Kanahā Beach is close to Kahului, where many of the windsurfing shops are located, thus making it a focal point for novice and intermediate windsurfers, who can launch and land safely along the wide sandy beach.

Kanahā Beach is also the best swimming beach on the Kahului/ Wailuku side of the island. With a gentle slope to overhead depths, it is a popular place for families and children.

*Kanahā* means "the shattered [thing]."

# Baldwin Beach Park

**Location:** On the Hāna Highway between the Maui Country Club and the town of Pāʻia.

**Activities:** Bodyboarding, bodysurfing, fishing, surfing, swimming.

**Description:** The long, wide, curving white sand beach fronting Baldwin Beach Park begins a half-mile away at Wawau Point, passes the Maui Country Club and the beach park, and ends at Kapukaulua Point. High, vegetated sand dunes form the back-shore, with ironwood trees being the primary vegetation. The dunes level off as they approach the beach park.

**Precautions:** This beach is subject to high surf that generates a powerful shorebreak and strong rip currents. The ocean bottom is sandy and drops quickly to overhead depths. Lifeguards are stationed here daily. Check with them before going in the water.

**Highlights:** This beach is regarded as one of the best shorebreak bodyboarding and bodysurfing sites on Maui. Some swimming occurs along the beach, but it is usually concentrated at the west end, where a large section of beachrock at the water's edge forms a shallow, sand-bottomed pool. The shorebreak surf at the beach park primarily attracts bodysurfers and bodyboarders. Some surfing also occurs at the point, where waves break offshore on a small reef. As one of the few shorebreak bodysurfing and bodyboarding sites on Maui, the park is often crowded, especially on weekends and holidays.

# Red Sand Beach

**Location:** Seaward side of Kaʻuiki Head, Hāna.

**Activities:** Snorkeling, swimming.

**Description:** Red Sand Beach is a pocket of red cinder sand in a cove on the east side of Kaʻuiki Head, the large headland on the shoreline of Hāna Bay. The beach is partially protected from the open ocean by a natural lava breakwater that extends across the mouth of the cove and forms a pool between the sand and the lava. The cove is enclosed by high sea cliffs. The trail that leads to the

beach begins between the Hāna School buildings and the Hotel
Hāna Maui's Sea Ranch Cottages.

**Precautions:** A narrow, sometimes precarious trail around the
east side of Ka'uiki Head is the only access to the beach. Go slowly
through the slide areas where the cinders are loose underfoot.
During periods of high surf, strong rip currents flow out of the
cove around the west end of the lava breakwater. At these times,
swim close to shore. This is a remote site with no lifeguards or any
other rescue assistance nearby.

The beach is located in a secluded cove and is used regularly by
nudists. If public nudity offends you, you may want to reconsider
visiting this beach.

**Highlights:** Ka'uiki Head is a volcanic cinder cone on the shoreline of Hāna Bay. While cinder cones are common on Hawaiian
shorelines, Ka'uiki Head is the only one with a high volume of red
cinder instead of the usual black. The red cinder is most prevalent
in the sea cliffs on the east side of the cone, where the raging seas
of the 'Alenuihāhā Channel have eroded it to form a beach in a
secluded cove. As the only red sand beach in Hawai'i, and one of
only a few in the world, Red Sand Beach is one of the geologically
unique beaches in the Hawaiian Islands. It is also one of Hawai'i's
most picturesque settings, with its red cinder beach and sea cliffs
covered with green ironwood trees, a black lava breakwater, and
clear, deep blue water.

The Hawaiian name of Red Sand Beach is *Kaihalulu,* "roaring
sea." *Ka'uiki,* the name of the cinder cone, means "the glimmer,"
and *'Alenuihāhā,* the name of the channel between Maui and the
Big Island, means "great, smashing waves."

# Mākena State Park

**Location:** South Kīhei Road, Mākena.

**Activities:** Bodyboarding, bodysurfing, fishing, snorkeling, surfing, swimming.

**Description:** Mākena State Park consists of two beaches that are popularly known as Big Beach and Little Beach. Big Beach, a white sand beach approximately 3,300 feet long and 100 feet wide, is bordered by fingers of lava to the southeast and by Puʻuōlaʻi, a volcanic cinder cone, to the northwest. Big Beach has a steep foreshore, the result of high surf that periodically strikes the beach.

Little Beach is a small cove with a wide, white sand beach between two lava points on the seaward side of Pu'uōla'i. The ocean bottom fronting the beach is a shallow sandbar with a normally gentle shorebreak. A short foot trail leads over the lava point that separates the two beaches. The lone amenity in the 160-acre park is a paved parking lot that is open during daylight hours only.

**Precautions:** High surf, particularly during the spring and summer months and during southerly (Kona) storms, generates dangerous shorebreak waves and powerful rip currents at Big Beach. Inexperienced swimmers and bodysurfers should stay on shore during these seasonal periods of high surf or they should walk over to Little Beach. Little Beach is also subject to high surf, but it is possible to wade and swim near shore during most surf conditions. This is a remote site with no lifeguards at either beach or any other rescue assistance nearby. If you are not experienced in high surf conditions, give every consideration to staying on shore until the surf subsides.

While state park regulations prohibit nudity, Little Beach continues to be one of Hawai'i's foremost nudist beaches. If public nudity offends you, you may want to reconsider visiting this beach.

**Highlights:** Big Beach and Little Beach are two of Maui's most popular bodysurfing and bodyboarding beaches. While Maui has many surfing and windsurfing sites, not many beaches have suitable waves for bodysurfing and bodyboarding. Big Beach is more for experienced wave riders, whereas Little Beach, with small, gentle waves breaking on a wide, shallow sandbar, is a good site for beginners. On calm days, snorkeling around the point separating the two beaches provides excellent viewing opportunities. Shorecasting, a form of pole fishing from sand beaches, is popular at Big Beach for *ulua,* or crevalle. These popular game fish may reach five feet in length and weigh over 100 pounds.

One of the most attractive features of the beach park is that it still has a feeling of wilderness, even though it is right at the edge of civilization. Big Beach is the longest, undeveloped white sand beach on Maui, so it attracts many people who are looking for a beach with no homes and no hotels. Only sand dunes covered with *kiawe* trees occupy the backshore.

The Hawaiian name for Big Beach is *Oneloa,* "long [stretch of] sand." *Puʻuōlaʻi,* the name of the cinder cone at the northwest end of the park, means "earthquake hill." *Mākena* means "abundance."

# Palauea Beach

**Location:** On Mākena Road at Palauea, immediately south of Polo Beach in Wailea.

**Activities:** Bodyboarding, bodysurfing, fishing, swimming.

**Description:** Palauea Beach is a wide, flat white sand beach approximately 1,500 feet long and 200 feet wide. Bordered at both ends by rocky points, the backshore consists of low dunes covered with *kiawe* primarily and *pōhuehue* (beach morning glory). The ocean bottom slopes gently across a shallow sandbar to overhead depths. Waves break occasionally on the sandbar.

**Precautions:** High surf generates dangerous water conditions, including a pounding shorebreak and powerful rip currents. No lifeguards are stationed here.

**Highlights:** Palauea Beach is one of the last undeveloped beaches on the Kīhei to Mākena shoreline, and, therefore, it is one of last secluded beaches on the leeward side of the island. It is an excellent swimming site under normal conditions, especially for families with little children, and because it is more recessed than other beaches nearby, it offers beachgoers more shelter from the prevailing winds. If you are looking for a beach near civilization that usually is not crowded, this is it.

On Saturday, May 8, 1994, normally deserted Palauea Beach was lined from end to end with hundreds of people when it became the site of a historic beachside ceremony. Shell horns and chanting opened the event that formally ended fifty-three years of military control of the island of Kahoʻolawe, located directly offshore from the beach and eight miles across the ʻAlalākeiki Channel. The signing of the title transfer documents took place between Undersecretary of the Navy William Cassidy, Jr., and Governor John Waihee at a table on the beach. Hundreds of spectators witnessed the signing. Afterward, everyone took part in a prayer that included grasping a ceremonial rope that ran the length of the beach with both ends anchored in the ocean. Chants and hula performances by Maui hālau concluded the event. The forty-five-square-mile island of Kahoʻolawe was taken over by the Navy in 1941 and used as a live firing training area until 1990. Protests against the bombing began in the 1960s and grew into a campaign of lawsuits and invasions of the island by Hawaiian rights activists who formed the Protect Kahoʻolawe ʻOhana. The ceremony marked the success of their efforts and the return of the island from federal to state control.

*Palauea* means "lazy."

# Wailea Beach

**Location:** Wailea Alanui Road, Wailea, fronting the Grand Wailea Resort Hotel and the Four Seasons Hotel.

**Activities:** Bodyboarding, bodysurfing, fishing, sailing, scuba diving, snorkeling, swimming, windsurfing.

**Description:** Situated between two points of lava, Wailea Beach is a wide pocket of white sand approximately 1,000 feet long and 200 feet wide. The inshore bottom is shallow and slopes gently across a sandbar to overhead depths. Inland of the beach are a landscaped minipark, restrooms, showers, and a paved parking lot. Public access to the beach is marked by a sign on Wailea Alanui Road.

**Precautions:** Dangerous water conditions occur during periods of high surf or during severe southerly (Kona) storms. No lifeguards are stationed here.

**Highlights:** Wailea Beach is the namesake of the Wailea Resort. *Wailea* means the "water [of] Lea," the goddess of Hawaiian canoe makers. Use of the name to include the entire resort began in the 1970s, when Alexander and Baldwin, Inc. (A&B) announced their proposal to develop a luxury resort community to be called Wailea. A&B is Maui's largest employer and the owner of the Hawaiian Commercial and Sugar Company (HC&S), the largest and one of the last sugar plantations in the state.

The beach is excellent for a variety of activities, especially swimming. It is the site of the annual Swim for Your Heart, a one-mile ocean swimming race that is a benefit for the Maui Chapter of the

American Heart Association. Swimmers negotiate a triangular course that begins and ends at Wailea Beach. When the ocean is calm, snorkeling is good around the rocky points at both ends of the beach, where green sea turtles and manta rays are common visitors. Humpback whales are also seen frequently during the winter months. Wave riding opportunities are good for bodysurfers and bodyboarders, and beach concessions at the hotels rent a variety of ocean recreation gear and offer instructions and tours.

# Ulua Beach

**Location:** Wailea Alanui Road, Wailea, between the Renaissance Wailea Beach Resort and the Aston Wailea Resort.

**Activities:** Bodyboarding, bodysurfing, kayaking, sailing, snorkeling, scuba diving, surfing, swimming, windsurfing.

**Description:** Ulua Beach is a wide pocket of white sand approximately 1,000 feet long and 200 feet wide and situated between two points of lava. The inshore bottom is shallow and slopes gently to the deeper waters off shore. During the winter months, high surf erodes the beach, often exposing cobblestones in the foreshore.

During the summer months, the sand returns, restoring the beach. Inland of the beach are a landscaped minipark, restrooms, showers, and a paved parking lot. Public access is marked by a sign on Wailea Alanui Road.

**Precautions:** Dangerous water conditions occur primarily during periods of high surf or during severe southerly (Kona) storms. No lifeguards are stationed here.

**Highlights:** Ulua Beach is the centermost of Wailea's five beautiful beaches, which from southeast to northwest are: Polo, Wailea, Ulua, Mōkapu and Keawakapu. When the ocean is calm, which is almost every day, snorkeling is excellent on the reef between Ulua and Mōkapu Beaches. Many Maui residents consider it to be one of the best snorkeling sites on the island. A second deeper reef, approximately 100 yards off shore, provides good viewing opportunities for scuba divers. Green sea turtles are common at both reefs, and humpback whales frequently transit the deeper waters beyond the reefs. Wave riding opportunities are good for body-surfers, bodyboarders, and occasionally board surfers during summer south swells. A full-service beach concession at the edge of the beach on the Renaissance Wailea Beach Resort property offers equipment rentals and scuba, snorkeling, kayaking, and windsurfing lessons.

*Ulua* is the Hawaiian name for the crevalle, a popular game fish that may reach five feet in length and weigh over 100 pounds. They frequent sand-bottomed areas in search of crabs and other food and are seen occasionally by snorkelers and scuba divers.

# Kāʻanapali Beach

**Location:** Fronting Kāʻanapali Resort, Hono a Piʻilani Highway, Kāʻanapali.

**Activities:** Bodyboarding, bodysurfing, fishing, kayaking, sailing, scuba diving, snorkeling, surfing, swimming, windsurfing.

**Description:** Kāʻanapali Beach fronts the entire Kāʻanapali Resort, extending more than two miles from Hanakaʻōʻō Beach Park in the south to Kahekili Beach Park in the north. It is accessed primarily from the two beach parks and from a number of public rights-of-way within the resort. Kekaʻa, or Black Rock, a volcanic cinder cone, rises above the center of the beach where it provides a unique pedestal for the Sheraton Maui. Beach concessions are located to the south at the Dig Me Beach Activity Center fronting Whalers Village and to the north at the West Maui Sailing School desk fronting the Aston Maui Kā'anapali Villas.

**Precautions:** Kā'anapali Beach on both sides of Black Rock is subject to high surf at all times of the year, but especially during the winter months. During periods of high surf, powerful waves pound the foreshore, creating a dangerous shorebreak with strong backwashes and swift rip currents. While personnel from the beach concessions perform ocean rescues if they spot someone in trouble in their area, they are neither hired nor trained as lifeguards. The nearest county lifeguard is stationed at Hanaka'ō'ō Beach Park at the south end of the resort. If you are not experienced in high surf conditions, give every consideration to staying on shore until the surf subsides.

**Highlights:** Among the hundreds of beaches in Hawai'i, Kā'anapali Beach is one of the few where you can find just about every form of ocean recreation that the islands have to offer. Swimming during no or low surf periods is excellent on either side of Black Rock. Snorkeling and scuba diving is outstanding at Black Rock and to the north fronting Kahekili Beach Park. Wave riding for bodyboarders and surfers is popular on the wide reef to the south, off the Maui Marriott Hotel. Sailing and windsurfing opportunities are found to the north fronting the Aston Maui Kā'anapali Villas. And Maui's highest density of sunbathers and socializers is found at Dig Me Beach, the section of Kā'anapali Beach fronting Whalers Village. Commercial boat tours are available at Whalers Village, too. In the midst of all these ocean activities, more passive beachgoers can find a number of restaurants and snack shops that offer shade, refreshments, and some great ocean views. If one-stop shopping for ocean recreation is what you want, Kā'anapali is the place for you.

*Kā'anapali* means "[land] division cliff." *Keka'a,* the Hawaiian name of Black Rock, means "the rumble."

# Kapalua Beach Park

**Location:** Lower Hono a Pi'ilani Highway, Kapalua.

**Activities:** Sailing, scuba diving, snorkeling, swimming.

**Description:** Kapalua Beach is a small pocket beach about 600 feet long and 100 feet wide that lies between two lava points. A large grove of coconut trees lines the backshore. The northern point extends into the prevailing winds and currents, protecting the beach from dangerous ocean conditions. Additional protection is provided at the southern point by several large rocks that act as a partial breakwater and by a coral reef that arcs toward the beach.

The ocean bottom slopes gently to overhead depths, creating a good area for swimming. A public beach park with parking, showers, and restrooms is located at the southern point of the bay. There are no lifeguards.

**Precautions:** Be cautious about venturing into the open ocean beyond the points of the bay, especially during periods of high surf, when longshore currents may be exceptionally strong.

**Highlights:** Kapalua Beach is one of the most picturesque beaches on Maui and has been a longtime favorite swimming and snorkeling site for visitors and residents. The protection provided by the two lava points on either side of the beach is an especially attractive feature for this part of the island, where every other beach is subject to the dangers of high winter surf. The sheltered bay attracts many families with little children who would otherwise have no where to swim safely in this area.

*Kapalua* means "two borders."

# Fleming Beach Park

**Location:** Hono a Piʻilani Highway, Honokahua Bay.

**Activities:** Bodyboarding, bodysurfing, surfing, snorkeling, swimming.

**Description:** Honokahua Beach, fronting Fleming Beach Park, is a straight 1,500-foot long and 150-foot wide white sand beach that lies between two lava points. Large ironwood trees dominate the low sand dunes in the backshore. The prevailing wind elevates the dunes near Makāluapuna Point, the south point of the bay. A shallow sandbar fronts most of the beach and extends offshore to the surf line, except at the east end, which is fronted by a shallow reef. The foreshore is steep, the result of the high winter surf sweeping across the beach. Facilities in Fleming Beach Park include restrooms, showers, and parking.

**Precautions:** During periods of high surf, especially during the winter months, a powerful shorebreak forms on the Fleming Beach Park sandbar, generating dangerous rip currents along the entire length of the beach. High surf may also generate a strong backwash across the sandbar. Lifeguards are on duty daily. Check with them before going in the water.

**Highlights:** Fleming Beach Park was named for David Thomas Fleming (1881–1955), a former manager of Honolua Ranch. Fleming introduced pineapple to West Maui as a commercial crop and converted the cattle ranch to a pineapple plantation. This was the beginning of Maui Land and Pineapple Company, an industry that continues today. Fleming's home, completed in 1915 and named Makaʻoiʻoi ("keen eyes"), is now the Pineapple Hill Restaurant.

Fleming Beach Park is situated on Honokahua Bay, one of the six famous bays of West Maui, which are collectively known as *Hono a Piʻilani* or the "bays [acquired] by [Chief] Piʻilani." The name of each bay begins with *"hono,"* or "bay," and in order from north to south they are Hononana ("animated bay"), Honokōhau ("bay drawing dew"), Honolua ("two bays"), Honokahua ("sites bay"), Honokeana ("cave bay"), and Honokōwai ("bay [for] drawing water").

Fleming Beach Park is the most popular bodysurfing and bodyboarding site on West Maui. Surf breaks almost daily on the sandbar fronting the park, even during the summer months, as long as the trade winds are blowing. This break attracts many visitors and residents. Occasionally, surf on the small reef at the east end of the beach is good enough for surfing.

# Moloka‘i

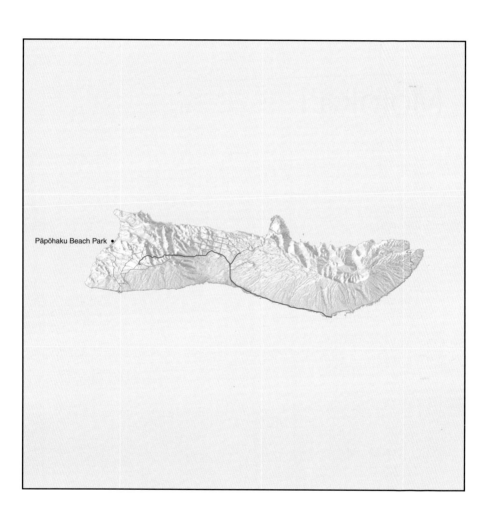

Pāpōhaku Beach Park •

# Pāpōhaku Beach Park

**Location:** West end of the island on Kaluakoʻi Road near the Kaluakoʻi Resort.

**Activities:** Bodyboarding, bodysurfing, snorkeling, surfing, swimming.

**Description:** Pāpōhaku Beach is a long, straight white sand beach over two miles long and up to 400 feet wide in its southern half. It lies between Puʻukoaʻe, a lava point to the south, and Puʻu o Kaiaka, a volcanic cinder cone to the north. The foreshore is steep, evidence of the high surf that regularly strikes the west side of the island. The backshore is lined by low, sparsely vegetated sand dunes. Under normal trade wind conditions, a longshore current flows from north to south.

Pāpōhaku Beach Park is located inland of the dunes at the north end of the beach. It has restrooms, showers, camping sites, and parking. Two other public rights-of-way to the beach are located east of the park along Kaluako'i Road, one in the middle at Lauhue Street and one at the south end at Pāpapa Street.

**Precautions:** Pāpōhaku Beach is subject to high surf at all times of the year. The entire beach is exposed to the open ocean, with no protective reefs or points to buffer the surf and longshore currents. Swimming is safe only during periods of no surf, primarily during the summer months. During periods of strong trade winds, stinging sand storms may sweep across the wide expanse of beach. No lifeguards are stationed here.

**Highlights:** Pāpōhaku Beach is one of the widest sand beaches in Hawai'i and the longest beach on Moloka'i. It is a great place to get away from civilization and wander along a deserted beach. Your only companions will be thousands of ghost crabs, whose burrows line the foreshore, and the myriad sea birds and occasional wild turkeys who feed on them. The beach is a good place to see the island of O'ahu, approximately twenty-five miles away across the Kaiwi Channel.

On calm, no surf days, you can swim and snorkel on the leeward side of Kaiaka Rock. On small surf days, bodysurfers and body-boarders ride several breaks along the beach. Pāpōhaku Beach is divided into three areas: Kaiaka Rock, adjacent to its namesake; Mid Rights in the middle; and Tunnels at the south end. Tunnels was named for the large concrete tunnel inland of the surfing site, the remnant of a former sand mining operation. Sand from Pāpō-haku Beach was hauled to Hale o Lono Harbor and shipped to O'ahu, where it was used by the construction industry. The tunnel on the beach allowed trucks to remove sand from below the high water mark, a common practice that was terminated in 1975 by state law.

Pāpōhaku Beach Park is the site of an annual hula festival called

Moloka'i Ka Hula Piko. It was established in 1991 by *kumu hula* John Keanuenue Ka'imikaua, founder of Hālau Hula o Kukunao-kalā, an academy that perpetuates the hula and other pre-Western Hawaiian traditions. The noncompetitive hula festival is held annually in May on Moloka'i's west end, where, according to Ka'i-mikaua, the hula was first taught before it spread throughout the islands. Moloka'i Ka Hula Piko, the name of the festival, refers to Moloka'i being the source, or *piko*, of the hula.

*Pāpōhaku* means "stone fence," *Pu'ukoa'e* means "tropic bird hill," and *Pu'u o Kaiaka* means "hill of Kaiaka [a mythical person]."

# Lāna'i

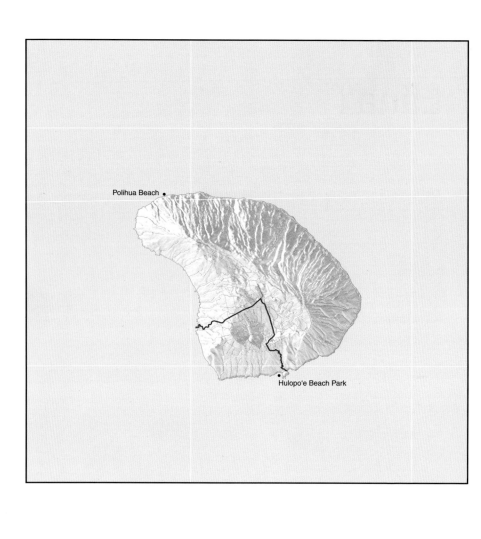

Polihua Beach

Hulopoʻe Beach Park

# Hulopoʻe Beach Park

**Location:** South coast of Lānaʻi, adjacent to the Mānele Bay Hotel.

**Activities:** Bodyboarding, bodysurfing, fishing, scuba diving, snorkeling, surfing, swimming.

**Description:** Hulopoʻe Beach is a pocket beach of white sand lying at the head of Hulopoʻe Bay. Approximately 1,500 feet long and 200 feet wide, it is bounded by lava points at each end. Low, vegetated dunes and a beach park occupy the backshore. The foreshore is steep from the force of high surf that strikes the beach, mostly during the summer. Amenities at Hulopoʻe Beach Park include paved parking, restrooms, showers, picnic tables, and a camping area. The park is privately owned by the Lāna'i Company.

**Precautions:** Camping in Hulopo'e Beach Park is by permit only. Permits are issued by the Lāna'i Company. Be sure to call ahead for reservations. Hulopo'e Bay, the waters fronting the beach, is part of the Mānele-Hulopo'e Marine Life Conservation District (MLCD). Fishing within the MLCD is restricted to hook and line fishing from shore. All other types of fishing, including gathering, are prohibited. The MLCD regulations also prohibit operating, anchoring, or mooring any vessel within Hulopo'e Bay. This means that the daily snorkeling and scuba diving charters from Maui must tie up in Mānele Boat Harbor and transport their guests overland from the harbor to Hulopo'e Beach in order to snorkel or dive there.

The Hulopo'e shorebreak is marginal for bodysurfing. The near-shore bottom drops quickly to overhead depths, creating poor shorebreak conditions for wave riding. Waves breaking over the shallow reef at the east end of the beach provide better opportunities for bodyboarding and surfing.

**Highlights:** Hulopo'e is the best swimming beach on the island, the only beach on the south shore, and the only beach conveniently accessible to all residents and visitors. The best snorkeling is between the eastern point of the beach and the center of the bay, where the reef is highly developed and fish are most evident. Hulopo'e Beach Park is the single most important shoreline recreation site on Lāna'i and is traditionally where the island's residents have gone to swim, fish, picnic, and camp, especially on weekends and holidays. It is only a fifteen-minute drive over paved roads from Lāna'i City. The rest of Lāna'i's beaches are at least an hour's drive from Lāna'i City over secondary roads, some of which require a vehicle with four-wheel drive.

Hulopo'e is also one of the few good surfing sites on Lāna'i and the only one on the island that is close to Lāna'i City and accessible by a paved road. It is heavily used by the resident bodyboarding and surfing community.

The meaning of *Hulopo'e* is unknown.

# Polihua Beach

**Location:** Northwest coast of Lānaʻi at the end of Polihua Road.

**Activities:** Bodyboarding, fishing, surfing, swimming.

**Description:** Polihua Beach, nearly two miles long and 350 feet wide, is the longest and widest white sand beach on the island. It borders Kalohi Channel, directly opposite the island of Molokaʻi. The foreshore is steep, the result of high surf that sweeps across the beach, and the ocean bottom drops steeply to overhead depths. The entire beach is exposed to the open ocean, with no protective reefs or points to buffer the surf and longshore currents. During periods of strong trade winds, stinging sand storms frequently sweep across the wide expanse of beach. For these reasons, most residents consider Polihua a wilderness fishing site rather than a recreational swimming beach. Access is possible only with a four-wheel-drive vehicle. The drive to Polihua takes an hour, first over a dirt road through the former pineapple fields and then down a rocky, rutted road to the beach. This road is subject to washouts and becomes impassable during periods of heavy rains.

**Precautions:** Ocean conditions may be dangerous because of high surf and strong currents. Vigorous trade winds may create sand storms that sweep across the beach. There are no facilities, no lifeguards, and no other rescue assistance nearby. Swim here only when the ocean is absolutely calm.

**Highlights:** Polihua Beach is a long, beautiful beach with an excellent view of Moloka'i. It is one of the few beaches left in Hawai'i where you can really get away from civilization and be alone. During the winter months, high surf sweeps several hundred feet inland over the sand, and humpback whales come within a stone's throw of shore. Polihua is not sheltered like Hulopo'e on the south shore, so swimming conditions are often marginal, but hiking north along the shoreline to Shipwreck Beach is an exciting and often productive beachcombing activity, especially during or immediately after high surf or a winter storm. Shipwreck Beach is famous for its vast arrays of flotsam and jetsam, including Japanese fishing floats or "glass balls," as they are known in Hawai'i.

*Polihua* means "eggs [in] bosom." The beach was once a famous nesting site for green sea turtles, and the name may refer to this former activity.

# Big Island

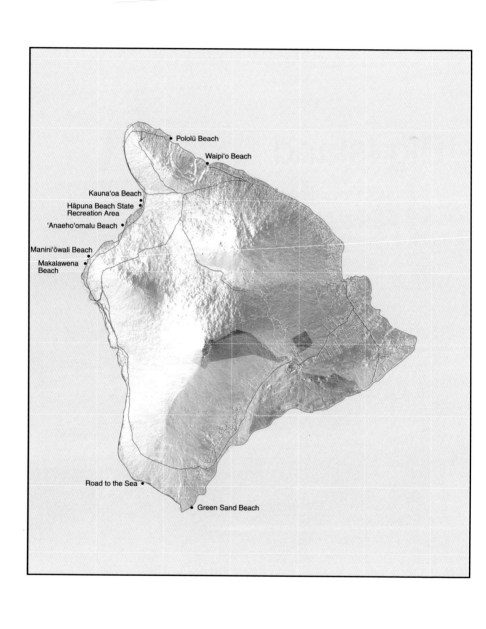

Pololū Beach

Waipiʻo Beach

Kaunaʻoa Beach

Hāpuna Beach State
Recreation Area

ʻAnaehoʻomalu Beach

Maniniʻōwali Beach

Makalawena
Beach

Road to the Sea

Green Sand Beach

# Green Sand Beach

**Location:** Near South Point. Follow South Point Road to Kaulana Boat Ramp. The beach is 2.5 miles east of the ramp over an unimproved dirt road.

**Activities:** Beachcombing, fishing, swimming.

**Description:** Green Sand Beach is a small pocket beach located at the base of Pu'u o Mahana, a littoral cinder cone that formed where a lava flow from Mauna Loa entered the ocean. The ocean bottom is sandy and slopes gently to overhead depths, providing good conditions for swimming. Waves penetrating the bay form a shorebreak the length of the beach. The beach is bordered by low lava sea cliffs.

High surf eroding the seaward face of Pu'u o Mahana washes out olivines, small green volcanic crystals, and deposits them on the beach below the cone. The veneer of olivines gives the beach its popular name.

**Precautions:** Green Sand Beach is located at the head of a narrow bay where it is subject to high surf at all times of the year. High surf generates a powerful shorebreak and dangerous rip currents and surges over the low rock ledges on both sides of the bay. Swim only when the ocean is calm. There are no lifeguards or any other rescue assistance nearby.

Hiking on Pu'u o Mahana, the hill above Green Sand Beach, especially across its seaward face, is dangerous because of the loose volcanic material underfoot.

The access road from the boat ramp to the beach is not passable in an ordinary passenger car. If you do not have a vehicle with four-wheel drive, park at the boat ramp and walk. Be sure to bring water and sunscreen.

**Highlights:** Olivines are commonly found in Hawaiian volcanic material, especially lava. In places where olivines are loosely embedded, such as in the ash and cinder of Pu'u o Mahana near South Point, they are easily separated from their parent material by wind, rain, and surf. Green Sand Beach is the most famous of all the green sand beaches in Hawai'i because it has an extremely high concentration of olivines. While most olivines are too small and imperfect to be considered as gem stones, many beachcombers continue to search for and occasionally find large individual crystals. The lure of gemstone-size olivines is one of the attractions of Green Sand Beach. In addition, the beach is located in a remote, isolated part of the Big Island that is definitely off the beaten path. The hike from Kaulana Boat Ramp and back through this stark but beautiful shoreline is worth the effort, especially with the beachcombing opportunities at the beach and in many little coves along the way.

# Road to the Sea

**Location:** Shoreline adjoining Humuhumu Point, Ka'ū. Follow the secondary cinder road called Road to the Sea seven miles to the ocean. Road to the Sea is located between Manukā State Park and the west boundary of Hawaiian Ocean View Estates subdivision. Most of the road is negotiable in an ordinary passenger car, but the last downhill slope to the shoreline requires a vehicle equipped with four-wheel drive. Park and walk down the final section of the road if you are driving an ordinary passenger car.

**Activities:** Fishing, hiking, snorkeling, swimming.

**Description:** Road to the Sea has two black sand beaches, one at Humuhumu Point and one at 'Āwili Point. Each beach has high concentrations of olivine in addition to the volcanic cinder, or "black sand," that comprises the bulk of the beach. The olivine concentration is enough on each beach to also call them "green sand" beaches. Both beaches have steep foreshores from the force of high surf striking them, and the ocean bottoms at each drop abruptly to overhead depths. Except for the two beaches, the shoreline is rocky, consisting of several lava flows and a series of cinder cones. At Keawaiki on the seaward side of Nā pu'u a Pele, a wide lava flat is pitted with many tidal pools, and small storm beaches are situated along the inner edge of the flat. Brackish water ponds are also found here along with some habitation sites of the former Keawaiki fishing village.

**Precautions:** Strong currents and high surf occur at all times of the year. High surf, particularly during the summer months and during southerly (Kona) storms, sweeps across both beaches, creating powerful shorebreaks and rip currents. During periods of high surf, waves also surge across the low lava points between the beaches. Be careful walking on the points and pay special attention when you are crossing areas that are already wet from the wash of previous waves. This is a remote, wilderness site where there are no lifeguards or any form of rescue assistance nearby. If your vehicle does not have four-wheel drive, park above the last hill down to the ocean. Be sure to bring sunscreen and drinking water.

**Highlights:** On the shoreline of Ka'ū, between South Point and Kaunā Point, lava flows from the southwest rift zone of Mauna Loa have entered the ocean many times. When molten lava pours into the ocean, violent steam explosions occur, ejecting tremendous amounts of volcanic debris. If this interaction continues for substantial periods of time, massive amounts of debris pile up at the edge of the flow, forming a cinder cone called a littoral cone. As the ocean erodes the loosely sorted material forming these cones, cinder sand beaches commonly form at their bases.

The largest concentration of littoral cones in Hawai'i is between

Humuhumu and 'Āwili Points, where the two highest are known as *Nā puʻu a Pele,* "the hills of Pele." According to Hawaiian legend, these hills were once two young chiefs who excelled in all sports, especially *hōlua,* or "sledding." Pele, goddess of the volcano, also loved this sport, and one day she appeared as a beautiful young chiefess to join in their competition. The chiefs, however, suspected her identity and refused to race with her. Angered, Pele chased them with a lava flow, overtaking them on the shoreline and turning them into the hills called Nā puʻu a Pele.

Nā puʻu a Pele is one of the most unique sections of volcanic shoreline in Hawaiʻi, with its dramatic blend of littoral cones, green and black sand beaches, storm beaches, rocky points, brackish water ponds, and tide pools. A network of shoreline trails leads from Road to the Sea to the scenic geographical features, including the summits of the Nā puʻu a Pele hills, and to the ruins of the former Keawaiki fishing village below them. The rocky points seaward of Nā puʻu a Pele are popular fishing sites for *ulua* (crevalle), which sometime weigh over 100 pounds. 'Āwili Point is especially well known for *ulua.* A number of camping sites are found there.

# Makalawena Beach

**Location:** Makalawena Beach is approximately four miles north of Keāhole Airport and one mile from Queen Ka'ahumanu Highway. It is most easily accessed by following the paved road to Mahai'ula Beach in Kekaha Kai State Park and then following the foot trail across Kāwili Point.

**Activities:** Bodyboarding, bodysurfing, fishing, scuba diving, snorkeling, surfing, swimming.

**Description:** The Makalawena shoreline consists of a long, curving white sand beach that slopes into a series of sandy coves separated by small points of lava. All of the coves are shallow and protected, providing good swimming areas. Dunes covered with *pōhuehue* (beach morning glory) and *kiawe (Prosopis pallida)* line the backshore at the south end of the beach. Inland of the beach is ʻŌpaeʻula Pond, a twelve-acre wetland that is an important habitat for the endangered Hawaiian stilt and other birds such as coots, ducks, night-crowned herons, plovers, tattlers, doves, mynahs, sparrows, and cardinals.

**Precautions:** The property inland of the beach is privately owned, so stay on the beach below the vegetation line to avoid trespassing. During the winter months, high surf generates dangerous water conditions, including strong longshore and rip currents. Swimmers and snorkelers should stay near shore during periods of high surf. Although the highway is only a mile away, this is a remote, undeveloped site with no lifeguards or any form of rescue assistance nearby. Be sure to bring sunscreen and drinking water with you.

**Highlights:** With its sandy coves and sand dunes and its long, curving beach, Makalawena is a great place near civilization to commune with nature. Of all the white sand beaches on the Kona coast, it is the least accessible from paved roads and, therefore, the least frequented. The south end of the beach offers excellent swimming. Snorkeling and scuba diving are popular off shore. During periods of high surf, surfers ride the waves off the north end of the beach. It may take a little effort to get here, but if solitude on a beautiful beach is what you want, you should visit Makalawena Beach.

*Makalawena* means "release [of] glow."

# Manini'ōwali Beach

**Location:** Approximately seven miles north of Keāhole Airport along Queen Ka'ahumanu Highway in Kekaha Kai State Park. Follow an unmarked secondary road immediately north of the eighty-eight-mile marker. From the intersection, it is approximately one mile to the beach. Some of the downhill sections of the road may not be passable in an ordinary passenger car. Park in the pull off areas close to the highway where other cars are parked.

**Activities:** Bodyboarding, bodysurfing, fishing, scuba diving, snorkeling, swimming.

**Description:** Manini'ōwali Beach is a large pocket of white sand approximately 650 feet long and fifty feet wide. Located at the head of Kua Bay and bordered by points of lava, it lies on the north side of Pu'u Kuili, a 342-foot-high cinder cone that is the most prominent natural landmark on the shoreline for many miles in either direction. The inland edge of the beach is bordered by a low wall of lava that varies in height from one to six feet. Several broken fingers of rock from the lava wall extend seaward, dividing the beach at its north and south ends and partially dividing the backshore into a series of smaller pockets of sand. At the north end of the beach, a gap between the lava wall and Papiha Point shelters a pocket of low sand dunes covered with *pōhuehue,* beach morning glory. A small, shallow brackish water pond immediately inland of the dunes serves as an occasional feeding site for the endangered Hawaiian stilt and other shorebirds.

A shallow sandbar normally fronts most of the beach, extending approximately fifty to seventy-five feet offshore. Waves break at the edge of the sandbar and roll ashore. High surf may severely erode the beach, submerging the beach to the level of the sandbar. At these times, pockets of dry sand are found only at the north and south ends of the beach. Once the high surf subsides, the sand begins to accrete and the beach is restored within one to two weeks. During the winter months, sand levels tend to remain lower because of the impact of consecutive periods of high surf.

**Precautions:** During periods of high surf, steep, plunging waves strike the beach, creating a dangerous shorebreak and powerful rip currents. These waves are for experienced wave riders only. Although the highway is only a mile away, this is a remote, undeveloped site with no lifeguards or any form of rescue assistance nearby. Be sure to bring sunscreen and drinking water with you.

**Highlights:** Manini'ōwali Beach is one of the Big Island's famous disappearing sand beaches. During periods of high surf, especially in the winter months from October to April, waves from a west or northwest direction scour the beach, severely eroding the sand and leaving only a remnant of the former beach. Sometimes as much as eight vertical feet of sand will be transported offshore in a twenty-four-hour period. A cave in the center of the lava wall on the backshore of the beach is used to gauge the severity of the sand erosion. Normally, the cave is almost completely filled with sand, but immediately after periods of high surf, an adult can stand erect inside with two feet of overhead clearance. The disappearance of the beach is a spectacular sight, especially combined with the immense waves that strike Papiha Point at the same time.

During periods of calm seas, Manini'ōwali is one of the best swimming beaches on the island because of its clear waters, clean, white sand, and small waves breaking on the shallow sandbar.

Visibility off Papiha Point is excellent for snorkeling and scuba diving. The underwater environment is spectacular, with small, rocky pinnacles and several deep underwater canyons, providing habitats for a wide variety of fish and invertebrates. Snorkelers may start at Manini'ōwali Beach, circle Papiha Point, and come ashore in the south corner of Kakapa Bay, the site of a small pocket of sand. From Kakapa Bay, follow the historic steppingstone trail across Papiha Point back to Manini'ōwali Beach. It is still paved in places with *pa'alā*, the smooth, flat, waterborne stones that are the traditional steppingstones used by Hawaiians for these types of trails. Be sure to bring footwear with you for the walk back.

*Manini'ōwali* is the name of a legendary princess. She was turned to stone at the water's edge, and the beach was named in her honor.

# 'Anaeho'omalu Beach

**Location:** South end of 'Anaeho'omalu Bay, adjacent to The Royal Waikoloan Hotel, Queen Ka'ahumanu Highway.

**Activities:** Kayaking, outrigger canoe paddling, scuba diving, snorkeling, surfing, swimming, windsurfing.

**Description:** 'Anaeho'omalu Beach, located at the head of 'Anaeho'omalu Bay, is approximately 900 feet long and 200 feet wide. Its sand has a speckled appearance because of nearly equal proportions of white and dark grains, the latter of which come from the lava that surrounds the bay. The beach is stable, experiencing little erosion or accretion throughout the year. The foreshore slopes back to a low, wave-cut bank, evidence of the high surf that strikes the outer regions of the bay during the winter months. The ocean bottom slopes gently to overhead depths. The backshore is flat, vegetated with an extensive coconut grove and bordered by two large ancient Hawaiian fishponds.

'Anaeho'omalu Beach Park is located at the south end of the beach. Its facilities include restrooms, showers, and parking.

**Precautions:** Although high surf strikes 'Anaeho'omalu Bay during the winter months, wave energy is dissipated by the outer reefs in the bay and does not pose a hazard for swimmers near shore. A small shorebreak may form onshore, but it normally does not generate any dangerous currents. During periods of high surf, however, any activities in the outer regions of the bay should be approached cautiously. There are no lifeguards at 'Anaeho'omalu Beach, but beachgoers may check with the staff at the Ocean Sports Waikoloa desk at the north end of the beach for water safety information. Swimmers should be alert to motor boat traffic at the north end of the beach and high-speed windsurfers at the south end of the beach during periods of strong winds.

**Highlights:** 'Anaeho'omalu Beach is the best one-stop center for ocean sports on the Big Island. With its beach, reefs, surfing sites, and winds, it offers almost every type of ocean recreation available in Hawai'i, including windsurfing. When the ocean is calm, the reef off 'Anaeho'omalu Point at the north end of the beach is a good snorkeling site, and when a northwest swell is running, it is a popular surfing site. Scuba tours to Pentagons and Pinnacles, two popular dive sites in the center of the bay, are conducted by the staff of Ocean Sports Waikoloa, a beach activities desk at the north end of the beach. In addition to the scuba tours, the beach desk rents a wide variety of equipment for all the activities in the bay and offers sound water safety advice to anyone who asks.

'Anaeho'omalu Beach is the best windsurfing site on the Big Island. It offers ideal nearshore conditions for beginners and challenging offshore conditions for high-performance windsurfing, including surfing and wave jumping. Novice windsurfers can take lessons and rent equipment from Ocean Sports Waikoloa, and expert windsurfers can easily get their equipment to the beach through the public beach park.

Swimmers and sunbathers looking for a more secluded beach site than ‘Anaeho‘omalu can visit Kapalaoa Beach on the south point of the bay. Follow the shoreline until you reach the long stretch of clean, white sand. The inshore bottom is rockier here, but the beach is normally deserted and the view inland is spectacular. An interesting archaeological site, a field of petroglyphs or Hawaiian rock drawings, is located in the lava flow just beyond the beach. No facilities are found at Kapalaoa Beach or in the petroglyph field.

*‘Anaeho‘omalu* means “restricted mullet,” a reference to the two fishponds behind the beach that were once maintained for the exclusive use of Hawaiian royalty traveling along the coast.

# Hāpuna Beach State Recreation Area

**Location:** Queen Kaʻahumanu Highway, South Kohala. Turn at the highway sign for the beach park.

**Activities:** Bodyboarding, bodysurfing, snorkeling, surfing, swimming.

**Description:** Hāpuna is a long, straight white sand beach, more than one-half mile in length, that lies between two lava points. During the summer months, the beach is over 200 feet wide, whereas during the winter months, high surf may erode the beach to half of its summer width. Midway along the beach, a lava ridge bisects the backshore. Hāpuna Beach State Recreation Area is located between the ridge and south point of the beach, and the Hāpuna Beach Prince Hotel is located between the ridge and the north point of the beach.

The foreshore of the beach slopes gently into a shallow sandbar that extends approximately twenty-five yards offshore. Waves breaking along the seaward edge of the sandbar form shorebreak surf that rolls up on shore. During the winter months when high surf strikes the beach, the shorebreak is especially powerful and generates dangerous rip currents.

Facilities in the beach park include camping shelters, pavilions, restrooms, showers, and parking.

**Precautions:** High surf striking the beach during the winter months produces a pounding shorebreak and powerful, shifting rip currents. Lifeguards are on duty every day of the year. Check with them before going in the water. State law prohibits surfing in the shorebreak, but during periods of high surf, surfers ride a deepwater break off the south point of the bay.

**Highlights:** Hāpuna is the widest white sand beach on the Big Island and one of its longest. The combination of beautiful beach, water activities, and well maintained public facilities has made Hāpuna the most popular beach on the Big Island. Residents from as far away as Hilo and Puna often drive here to picnic and to spend the day, especially on weekends and holidays.

The shorebreak at Hāpuna is the most popular bodysurfing and bodyboarding site on the Big Island. Wave riders come here from all over the island.

During the calm summer months, Hāpuna is the site of the Big Island's Rough Water Swim, an annual event since 1979. The roughly circular 1.1 mile course uses the entire width of the bay and attracts a number of swimmers from other islands.

*Hāpuna* means "spring."

# Kauna'oa Beach

**Location:** Fronting the Mauna Kea Beach Hotel.

**Activities:** Bodyboarding, bodysurfing, snorkeling, surfing, swimming.

**Description:** Kauna'oa Beach is a flat white sand beach, approximately 2,500 feet long and 200 feet wide, that is located between two points of lava. Its foreshore has a gentle slope, and the ocean bottom slopes gently to overhead depths. The backshore is vegetated, primarily by *naupaka*. Public facilities adjacent to the hotel include restrooms, showers, and parking, all of which are located at the south end of the beach.

**Precautions:** High surf strikes the beach during the winter months, producing a pounding shorebreak and powerful, shifting rip currents. No lifeguards are on duty, but hotel beach attendants do double duty as lifeguards when necessary. Check with them before going in the water if you have any doubts about the safety of the water conditions.

**Highlights:** As one of the most beautiful white sand beaches on the Big Island, Kauna'oa Beach was a logical site for Laurance S. Rockefeller to build the Mauna Kea Beach Hotel. Completed in 1965, it was the first of the major resorts on the west coast of the Big Island between Kailua and Kawaihae. Today, Kauna'oa Beach remains unchanged and is still a favorite of visitors and residents. Bodysurfing and bodyboarding are popular in the shorebreak, and during periods of high surf, several surfing sites form in the outer bay. On calm days, snorkelers are commonly seen puttering around the rocky points at either end of the beach.

*Kauna'oa* is the name of a plant, the dodder, and the name of a mollusk, the tube shell (family Vermetidae).

# Pololū Beach

**Location:** At the end of Highway 270, North Kohala.

**Activities:** Beachcombing, bodyboarding, fishing, surfing, swimming.

**Description:** Pololū Valley, the northernmost of seven coastal valleys on the north side of Kohala Mountain, is fronted by a curving black sand beach approximately 1,200 feet long and 125 feet wide. The "black sand" grains are lava fragments that have been eroded from Kohala Mountain and transported into the ocean at the north end of the beach by Pololū Stream. The ocean has redeposited the grains on shore at the mouth of the valley to form Pololū Beach, and the prevailing trade winds have blown them inland to form a bank of high dunes in the backshore. Large ironwood trees are the primary vegetation on the dunes.

A wide sandbar extends offshore approximately 200 feet, generating an almost continuous shorebreak along its seaward edge. Rip currents are common along the length of the beach. The beach is accessed by hiking the trail that begins at the Pololū Lookout and ends below at the mouth of the stream.

**Precautions:** Pololū Beach is a remote, isolated beach that is exposed to high surf throughout the year, but especially during the winter months. Strong longshore and powerful rip currents are a constant danger to all swimmers. There are no lifeguards or any other rescue assistance nearby. Do not swim in the ocean if the conditions are rough or if the surf is up.

**Highlights:** Of the seven beautiful coastal valleys in Kohala, Pololū is the most easily accessible. A fifteen-minute walk down an ancient Hawaiian switchback trail leads to the beach and the mouth of Pololū Stream. After storms or periods of high surf, the debris line is often a beachcomber's delight, littered with flotsam and jetsam from the open ocean and occasionally including a Japanese fishing float, or "glass ball," as they are called in Hawai'i.

At one time, taro was cultivated in Pololū and all of the other Kohala valleys, but today, except for Waipi'o, the valleys are uninhabited, and the taro patches are overgrown with introduced vegetation. The attraction for visitors now is the isolation and tranquility that the beach affords on almost any day of the year.

A *pololū* is a long, hardwood spear.

# Waipiʻo Beach

**Location:** At the end of Highway 240, North Hāmākua.

**Activities:** Beachcombing, bodyboarding, fishing, surfing.

**Description:** Waipiʻo Valley, the southernmost of seven coastal valleys on the north side of Kohala Mountain, is fronted by a curving black sand beach approximately 4,000 feet long and 200 feet wide. The "black sand" grains are lava fragments that have been eroded from Kohala Mountain and transported into the ocean at the south end of the beach by Waipiʻo Stream. The ocean has redeposited the grains on shore at the mouth of the valley to form

Waipiʻo Beach, and the prevailing trade winds have blown them inland to form an extensive series of dunes in the backshore on both sides of the stream. Large ironwood trees are the primary vegetation on the dunes.

A long, broad, shallow sandbar extends offshore approximately 250 feet, generating an almost continuous shorebreak along its seaward edge. The sandbar dissipates some of the wave energy from the shorebreak surf before it rolls on shore, but rip currents are common along the length of the beach.

**Precautions:** Waipiʻo Beach is a remote, isolated beach that is exposed to high surf throughout the year, but especially during the winter months. Strong longshore and powerful rip currents are a constant danger to all swimmers. There are no lifeguards or any other rescue assistance nearby. Do not swim in the ocean if the conditions are rough or if the surf is up.

The only road into Waipiʻo Valley is long, narrow, and extremely steep, hugging the valley wall as it descends. Only vehicles with four-wheel drive are allowed over it, and downhill traffic must yield to uphill traffic. Do not attempt this road in an ordinary passenger car. A commercial shuttle service at the lookout offers tours of the valley.

**Highlights:** Waipiʻo Valley is one of the most famous and beloved places in the Hawaiian Islands. Its natural beauty, spectacular waterfalls, historical importance, and mythological associations have made it a source of inspiration for writers, composers, and poets, in whose works the name Waipiʻo has been extolled and perpetuated. Waipiʻo Valley was once heavily populated with Hawaiians and was a favorite home of some of the Big Island's important chiefs. The valley floor was the greatest wetland taro valley on the island and one of the largest planting areas in the eight major islands. Today, only a few people live permanently in Waipiʻo and only a small fraction of the land is still cultivated, primarily by taro farmers who commute from their homes outside the valley. Many of the *loʻi*, or taro patches, are still visible from Waipiʻo Lookout, but most of them are overgrown by guava and other introduced vegetation. During the twentieth century, out-migration, transportation problems, severe flooding, and tsunami all played a part in the demise of the valley's taro production. The scenic valley remains, however, a popular destination for residents and visitors.

Waipi'o is a unique black sand beach because the lava fragments have been transported here by Waipi'o Stream, not by the ocean. The volume of stream-carried "sand" is so great that it has formed the longest beach, the longest sandbar, and the most extensive dunes on the Big Island.

Most residents consider the shorebreak too dangerous for swimming, but bodyboarders and surfers often ride the waves off shore. On no surf days, swimming takes place close to shore on the south side of Waipi'o Stream. The beach is great for beachcombing. It is one of the few places on the Big Island where you can still find "glass balls," hand-blown glass Japanese fishing floats that occasionally wash up on shore after severe storms or during periods of high surf. The dunes on the south side of the stream are a popular camping site.

Even if you choose not to get in the water, a trip through the valley is well worth the time.

*Waipi'o* means "curved water."

# Kaua'i

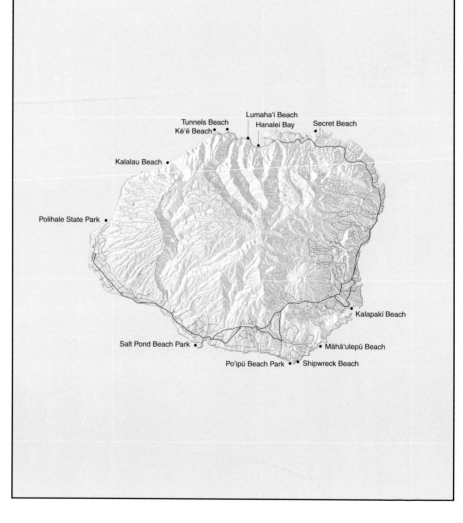

Tunnels Beach
Kēʻē Beach

Lumahaʻi Beach
Hanalei Bay

Secret Beach

Kalalau Beach

Polihale State Park

Kalapakī Beach

Salt Pond Beach Park

Māhāʻulepū Beach

Poʻipū Beach Park

Shipwreck Beach

# Kalapakī Beach

**Location:** Fronting the Kauaʻi Marriott Resort and Beach Club on Nāwiliwili Bay, Līhuʻe.

**Activities:** Bodyboarding, bodysurfing, outrigger canoe surfing, fishing, sailing, snorkeling, surfing, swimming, windsurfing.

**Description:** Kalapakī Beach is a white sand beach, approximately 1,300 feet long and 150 feet wide, located on the north side of Nāwiliwili Bay. It lies between a sea cliff to the east and a seawall to the west. Nāwiliwili Stream crosses the west end of the beach. The ocean bottom slopes gently across a shallow sandbar. Occasionally, waves break at the seaward edge of the sandbar and roll onshore.

Public parking, showers, and restrooms to the rear of the beach have been provided by the Kaua'i Marriott Resort and Beach Club. Public access is also available from Nāwiliwili Park at the west end of the beach. There are no lifeguards.

**Precautions:** Kalapakī Beach is tucked into a corner of Nāwiliwili Bay where it is well protected from the open ocean. Under normal surf conditions, there are no dangerous currents at the beach. High surf from the east or south, however, may enter the bay and break at the beach, generating rip currents in the nearshore areas. High surf also attracts bodyboarders and board surfers, and there is often a congested mixture of wave riders all vying for the same waves. Inexperienced bodyboarders and board surfers need to be careful in the crowds when the surf is up.

**Highlights:** Kalapakī Beach is one of the island's most popular and heavily used beaches. As the closest sand beach to the Kaua'i Marriott Resort and Beach Club and to Lihu'e, the population center of the island, it is a favorite with visitors and residents. The surfing site at the beach is an ideal beginner's break, with gentle waves that roll across a shallow sandbar, and it is well used during any sizable swell in the bay. During periods of favorable winds, twin-hull sailors and windsurfers sail in the bay, using the beach as an entry and exit point. Kalapakī Beach is a pleasant surprise in a bay that also has a small boat and a commercial boat harbor. Its protected location makes it a great place for families with small children. Two shopping centers at the west end of the beach, Anchor Cove and Pacific Ocean Plaza, offer a variety of restaurants and shops.

*Kalapakī* means "the ti ridge."

# Māhāʻulepū Beach

**Location:** Māhāʻulepū, east of the town of Kōloa. Take Kōloa Road to Weliweli Road and pass San Raphael Church. Follow Māhāʻulepū Road three miles past the Kōloa sugar mill to the shoreline. Māhāʻulepū is owned by Grove Farm Company, and access to the beach is across their property. The company permits the public to use the beach seven days a week during daylight hours from sunup to sundown, but the gates are locked at night.

**Activities:** Bodyboarding, fishing, snorkeling, surfing, swimming, windsurfing.

**Description:** The Māhā'ulepū shoreline stretches for two miles between Kawelikoa Point to the east and Kāmala Point to the west and includes a series of bays, coves, and white sand beaches. The ocean bottom offshore the beaches is mostly shallow with alternating patches of sand and rock.

**Precautions:** Strong currents and high surf may occur at any time of the year, but especially during the summer months. There are no lifeguards or facilities in this remote, undeveloped area. Since public access is permitted only during the day, be sure you leave before dark. The landowner provides security patrols to ensure that everyone observes the visiting hours.

**Highlights:** Māhā'ulepū is one of the most scenic sections of Kaua'i's south shore. It is also an important area geologically, biologically, and archaeologically. Shoreline geological features include lithified dunes, raised coral reefs, wave-cut terraces, sea cliffs, and a sea stack. The dunes harbor fossil remains of extinct birds, including three species of goose, a long-legged owl, and a flightless rail. Flocks of seabirds gravitate to the beaches and to several ponds and siltation basins. A colony of wedge-tailed shearwaters nests on one of the cliff faces. The dunes support a variety of native strand vegetation and several stands of large ironwood trees. Caves nearby contain two rare insects, a blind wolf spider and a blind terrestrial amphipod. Historians have also reported that many precontact archaeological sites were probably destroyed when the Māhā'ulepū lands were cleared for the cultivation of sugarcane. The remaining sites, including burials in the dunes, indicate that the area was once well populated.

In addition to the features of historical and scientific interest, Māhā'ulepū is an important area for all types of ocean recreation activities and provides one of the few windsurfing sites on Kaua'i's south shore. Beachgoers frequent the entire two-mile stretch of shoreline, but Kawailoa Bay in the center of Māhā'ulepū is the most popular site. Its shoreline consists of a white sand beach and a low, limestone sea cliff.

*Māhā'ulepū* means "and falling together."

# Shipwreck Beach

**Location:** In Poʻipū fronting the Hyatt Regency Kauaʻi Resort and Spa, 1571 Poʻipū Road.

**Activities:** Bodyboarding, bodysurfing, fishing, surfing, swimming, windsurfing.

**Description:** Shipwreck Beach is a white sand beach, approximately 2,500 feet long and 100 feet wide, that lies between Maka-wehi and Makahūʻena Points. Low-lying rocks line most of the beach, except at the east end, where the foreshore is sandy. The ocean bottom drops quickly to overhead depths. Small trade wind-generated surf breaks constantly throughout the year on a reef offshore Makawehi Point, and seasonal summer surf breaks offshore the east end of the beach. Public facilities on the east side of the Hyatt Regency Kaua'i Resort include restrooms, showers, and parking.

**Precautions:** High surf, especially during the summer months, generates powerful rip currents at the swimming beach and throughout the bay. No lifeguards are stationed here, so check with the resident surfers for conditions before going in the water. The Hyatt Regency Kaua'i Resort uses a flag warning system for its guests, with red indicating dangerous conditions. Check for the color of their flag.

**Highlights:** Shipwreck Beach is one of the most popular sites on Kaua'i for bodysurfing and bodyboarding. Its fast-breaking summer surf attracts wave riders from all over the island, including members of the South Shore Bodysurfing Club. Board surfers and windsurfers ride the waves on the wide reef offshore Makawehi Point, while *ulua* fishermen cast their lines from the top of the point. The long beach is popular with walkers, who enjoy the scenery, the activity in the surf, and hiking to the top of the point.

Shipwreck Beach takes its name from an unnamed wooden boat that lay on the sand at the water's edge for many years. It was battered by storms and stripped of its decking by people hunting firewood, but survived these assaults until November 23, 1982. On that day Hurricane 'Iwa struck Kaua'i and destroyed what little remained of the shipwreck. Today, only its heavy, rusted motor remains, buried in the sand, where it is occasionally exposed during periods of high surf.

Exceptionally high surf also exposes slabs of beachrock that, like the remains of the shipwreck, are normally buried under the sand. A field of petroglyphs carved into the beachrock by ancient Hawaiians is considered a historic site and attracts many visitors during the rare occasions when it is visible.

*Keoneloa,* the Hawaiian name of the beach, means "the long sand [stretch of]."

# Po'ipū Beach Park

**Location:** On Ho'owili Road off of Po'ipū Beach Road, Po'ipū.

**Activities:** Bodyboarding, fishing, snorkeling, surfing, swimming.

**Description:** Po'ipū Beach is a white sand beach approximately 1,100 feet long and fifty feet wide. The eastern half of the beach is backed by Po'ipū Beach Park and the western half by several hotels. A small boulder breakwater forms a protected swimming area in front of the beach park. Nukumoi Point, in the center of the beach, is a tombolo, a sandbar that joins a shallow rock islet to the beach. The sandbar is emergent at low tide, and the ocean bottom slopes gently to overhead depths on either side of it.

On the east side of the point, surf breaks on a shallow sandbar. On the west side, surf breaks on a submerged reef.

Facilities in the beach park include restrooms, showers, and parking.

**Precautions:** Po'ipū Beach is subject to seasonal high surf, especially during the summer months. During periods of high surf, rip currents run through both of the surfing sites. Lifeguards are stationed at the beach park. Check with them before going in the water.

**Highlights:** Po'ipū Beach, the most popular beach park on Kaua'i's south shore, is heavily used by visitors and residents. This beach has something for everyone: a protected swimming area for families with little children, a bodyboarding site directly in front of the park for older children and novice adults, a surfing site for experienced surfers, and a good reef for snorkeling. Hawaiian monk seals regularly come to rest and bask in the sun at Nukumoi Point.

*Po'ipū* means "completely overcast" or "crashing," as waves.

# Salt Pond Beach Park

**Location:** West of Pūʻolo Point, Hanapēpē.

**Activities:** Bodyboarding, fishing, scuba diving, snorkeling, surfing, swimming, windsurfing.

**Description:** Salt Pond Beach is a wide pocket of white sand that lies between two rocky points. A natural ridge of rock in the ocean joins the two points, creating a large saltwater pool between the beach and the ridge. The ridge is broken in many places, providing good circulation in the pool. Beyond the beach and ridge is a wide expanse of reef. Seasonal surf forms on the reef.

Facilities include restrooms, showers, picnic pavilions, and parking.

**Precautions:** During periods of high surf, potentially dangerous rip currents form in the openings of the natural ridge. Swim nearshore if the surf is up. There are no lifeguards stationed here.

**Highlights:** Salt Pond Beach Park attracts many families with children to its protected, pool-like swimming area. It is also a popular surfing and windsurfing site. Surfers ride several breaks on the reef, and the prevailing trade winds provide good conditions for windsurfers. During periods of calm seas, snorkelers and scuba divers also frequent the reef.

Salt Pond Beach Park is unique in Hawai'i not so much for its ocean recreation activities as for its rock salt, salt that is produced when sea water evaporates in small, shallow ponds adjacent to the beach. This traditional method of making salt has been practiced here for many years and has changed little since precontact times.

Saltmaking is a summer activity that is dependent on extended periods of dry weather and hot sun. Rain disrupts the process and dilutes or dissolves the drying salt. Saltmaking begins in May when the ponds are cleaned of debris and filled with salt water. After several days the water evaporates, leaving crystallized salt in its place. The salt is raked into a mound in the pond and allowed to drain briefly. It is then removed and stored under cover where it can drain and dry completely. The final product is bagged and used as needed. The process is repeated continuously throughout the summer.

Most of the ponds at Salt Pond Beach Park are supervised by Hui Hana Pa'akai, an organization whose members are permitted by the state to manufacture salt there. Most of the group's members have been working these ponds since they were children, continuing a tradition that was practiced by their forebears and handed down to them. The salt they make is for home consumption and is not a commercial product.

# Polihale State Park

**Location:** West end of Kaumualiʻi Highway, Kekaha.

**Activities:** Bodyboarding, surfing, swimming, windsurfing.

**Description:** Polihale Beach is a wide white sand beach approximately three miles long and 300 feet wide. It begins at Nohili Point, where the backshore consists of vegetated dunes that are 100 feet high, and ends at the Polihale sea cliffs. A wide sandbar extends several hundred yards offshore at the west end of beach. Surf breaks almost constantly on the sandbar.

**Precautions:** High surf during the winter months creates powerful rip currents, often right at the water's edge, where the ocean bottom may drop abruptly to overhead depths. These currents regularly sweep unsuspecting swimmers into the surf and have been the cause of many drownings over the years. This side of the island is also known for its large tiger sharks. The last shark attack in the area occurred on October 28, 1997, at the Pacific Missile Range Facility (PMRF), the military base adjacent to Polihale Beach Park. An eighteen-year-old bodyboarder lost his right foot in the attack but otherwise survived. Be careful swimming here. Remember that this is a remote beach with no lifeguards or any other rescue assistance nearby.

**Highlights:** Polihale Beach is one of the widest beaches in Hawai'i and one of the longest. It also has the highest and most famous dunes of any beach in the islands. Known as the Barking Sands, the dunes emit noises like a barking dog when they are agitated. In 1875, the Barking Sands were described in a letter from a resident of Honolulu to the California Academy of Sciences as follows:

> If you slap two handfuls of the sand together, a sound is produced like the hooting of an owl. If a person kneels on the steep incline, and then, with the two hands extended and grasping as much sand as possible, slides rapidly down, carrying all the sand he can, the sound accumulates till it is like distant thunder. But the greatest sound we produced was by having one native lie upon his belly, and another take him by the feet and drag him rapidly down the incline. With this experiment the sound was terrific, and could have been heard many yards away.

Barking sands, or singing sands, as they are called in other parts of the world, have been identified in the Sinai Desert in Egypt, the Gobi Desert in Mongolia, the Atacama Desert in Chile, and the Empty Quarter in Saudi Arabia. In addition to the Barking Sands site at Polihale, Hawaiians identified two other such sites, one at 'Ōhikilolo on O'ahu and one at Kaluakahua on Ni'ihau. Generically, each of the sites was called *ke one kani*, "the musical sands."

Fronting the dunes, midway along Polihale Beach, is a small

section of reef at the water's edge. Local residents call it Queen's Pond. When the ocean is calm, especially during the summer months, this little reef provides a quiet, protected swimming area that is well used by families with children. Queen's Pond is the best and safest swimming site on Polihale Beach. When southerly, or Kona, winds are strong, the reef is also a popular launching and landing site for windsurfers.

*Polihale* means "house bosom," but the meaning of the translation is unknown.

# Kalalau Beach

**Location:** Kalalau Beach is located in Nā Pali Coast State Park at the foot of Kalalau Valley. It can be reached by hiking the Kalalau Trail, an eleven-mile trail that begins at Kēʻē Beach at the end of Highway 56. A commercial boat tour company also offers several options: they will ferry you in, they will drop off your equipment on the beach while you hike the trail, or they will ferry you out. In addition, several kayak tour companies rent kayaks to those who would like to paddle in and out.

**Activities:** Beachcombing, bodyboarding, bodysurfing, fishing, kayaking, snorkeling, surfing, swimming.

**Description:** Kalalau is the largest of the five major white sand beaches located within Nā Pali Coast State Park. It is over 2,000 feet long and approximately 200 feet wide. Beach width varies considerably depending on the time of year. In the winter, it narrows, and during the summer, it widens. The backshore consists of vegetated dunes, the site of most of the park's camp sites. Off shore, the ocean bottom drops quickly to overhead depths on a wide sandbar that fronts most of the beach. Surf forms on the sandbar, especially during the winter months. Boulders at the water's edge front the east end of the beach. The west end terminates at a sea cliff indented by several large sea caves at its base.

**Precautions:** All of the beaches in the Nā Pali Coast State Park are subject to high surf at all times of the year, but especially during the winter months. High surf generates swift longshore currents, powerful rip currents, and a pounding shorebreak, all dangerous conditions for swimmers. Swimming is safest during the normally surf-free summer months. Keep in mind that you are in a wilderness park and a long way from professional rescue assistance. If you are in doubt about the safety of the ocean conditions, check with the park ranger.

During periods of heavy rains, flash floods occur in the park without warning. Do not cross a stream that has flooded. Wait for the water to subside.

Nā Pali Coast State Park is managed by the Division of State Parks. Permits are required for camping anywhere in the park and for hiking beyond Hanakāpīʻai, the first beach and valley on the Kalalau Trail. Do not hike into Kalalau without a permit, or you will be asked to leave.

**Highlights:** Kalalau is the most famous shoreline hiking destination in Hawaiʻi. Every year hundreds of hikers from all over the world come to Kauaʻi to experience the isolated beauty of Kalalau in the heart of the Nā Pali Coast State Park, 6,500 acres of exceptionally beautiful scenery. *Nā Pali* means "the cliffs" and refers to the fifteen miles of majestic sea cliffs between Kēʻē and Polihale Beaches. Nā Pali's coastal wilderness provides excellent opportunities for hiking, backpacking, camping, swimming, and snorkel-

ing. Most campers hike to Kalalau, but some elect to paddle in kayaks or ride on shuttle boats.

If you do not have the time or inclination to backpack into Kalalau, day excursions on commercial boats along the Nā Pali coast are some of the most exciting tours Hawai'i has to offer. Most of them include a snorkeling stop at Nu'alolo Kai, another beach to the west of Kalalau that has an extensive coral reef. This is a tour that every visitor and resident should take at least once. Commercial tours along the Nā Pali coast were started in 1977 by Captain Zodiac, who is still one of the major tour operators.

During the summer months, a popular swimming excursion from Kalalau is a visit to Honopū Beach, immediately beyond the west point of Kalalau. Honopū can only be reached by water, so if you are a good swimmer and equipped with a pair of fins, you can get there in twenty minutes. Park regulations prohibit beach landings at Honopū by boats, including kayaks, but boaters can anchor off shore and swim in. Again, do not forget your fins. Honopū is one of the most picturesque beaches in the Hawaiian islands and one of the most photographed by air. You will not regret making the extra effort to get there.

From a distance, Honopū's twin pocket beaches of white sand are seemingly separated by a high, narrow ridge of lava that extends into the ocean, but upon closer inspection you will see that the beaches are actually connected through a high sea arch in the ridge. In the midst of the sand and the sea cliffs, a waterfall emerges from the valley above and flows through the arch into the ocean. This is a perfect Hawaiian beach, minus the palm trees.

*Kalalau* means "the straying," and *Honopū* means "conch bay."

# Kē'ē Beach

**Location:** Kē'ē Beach is located in Hā'ena State Park at the west end of Highway 56.

**Activities:** Fishing, snorkeling, swimming.

**Description:** Hā'ena State Park lies between Limahuli Stream to the east and Nā Pali Coast State Park to the west. The western end of the park is fronted by Kē'ē Beach, a narrow white sand beach that parallels a wide, shallow reef flat. A small, sand-bottomed lagoon lies off the west end of the beach. A deep, narrow channel through the reef joins the lagoon to the open ocean. Many large ironwood trees, some with their roots exposed, line the backshore.

**Precautions:** Kē'ē Beach is exposed to high surf winter months and occasionally during the summer mo surf activity is evidenced in the backshore by the severe ꞏ ꞏꞏon of the dunes, where waves sweeping across the beach have undermined the ironwood trees, exposing their roots and occasionally toppling them onto the beach. High surf also generates a powerful rip current that runs out the narrow channel at the west end of the lagoon to the open ocean. Swimmers and snorkelers should stay clear of the channel at any time there is a rip current, which is any time surf is breaking on the reef. There are no lifeguards here.

**Highlights:** Kē'ē Beach is the most popular snorkeling site on Kaua'i's north shore. Visitors drive from all parts of the island to snorkel in the small, protected lagoon off the beach, where many species of colorful reef fish are abundant, including wrasses, butterflyfish, damselfish, goatfish, convictfish, and surgeonfish. The shallow, sandy lagoon also provides an excellent swimming area for families with little children.

Kē'ē Beach is one of the most tropical looking beaches on Kaua'i with its high mountains and lushly vegetated backshore. Ironwoods line the dunes, and coconut palms, tropical almonds, and a dense undergrowth of *ti* and guava cover the point at the west end of the beach. In the midst of this tropical splendor are several important archaeological sites associated with the hula, including Ke Ahu o Laka, a platform where the hula is performed, and Kauluapaoa Heiau, a temple dedicated to Laka, the goddess of the hula. These sites are still used by *hula hālau* for graduation and other ceremonies.

*Kē'ē* means "avoidance."

# Tunnels Beach

**Location:** At Hāʻena Point approximately one-half mile east of Hāʻena Beach Park.

**Activities:** Beachcombing, bodyboarding, fishing, scuba diving, snorkeling, surfing, swimming, windsurfing.

**Description:** Tunnels Beach is a section of the long, winding white sand beach at Hāʻena. It is approximately 2,500 long and 200 feet wide and fronts Hāʻena Point, where much of the foreshore is lined by beachrock. Off shore is Mākua Reef, a massive, hook-shaped reef that contains a deep lagoon within its hook. A wide channel,

Mākua Channel, leads into the lagoon from the west, and a narrow channel, Kanahā Channel, leads into it from the east.

Tunnels is accessible from two public rights-of-way, one on each side of Hā'ena Point, but parking at each is limited. These rights-of-way were intended primarily to provide pedestrian beach access for area residents who do not live on the beach, not to accommodate the public and their vehicles. Tunnels is best reached by parking at Hā'ena Beach Park and walking east. The beach park is also the only place in the neighborhood where public restrooms and showers are available.

**Precautions:** During periods of high surf, strong rip currents run though the lagoon and out both Mākua and Kanahā Channels. High surf also sweeps across the beach. Unless you are an expert surfer or windsurfer, stay out of the water during periods of high surf. There are no lifeguards here or at the beach park.

Kanahā Channel is a primary entry and exit point for windsurfers. Swimming and snorkeling here are not advisable if windsurfers are using the area. They come in and out of the beach at high rates of speed, and a collision with one of them would be painful.

**Highlights:** Tunnels takes its name from the arches and tunnels that are found in the lagoon on the inside of Mākua Reef. These underwater features and the wide variety of fish in them have made the beach a popular snorkeling and scuba diving destination. Scuba divers especially like Tunnels because it offers them a moderately deep dive (approximately fifty feet) in a protected area that is easily accessible from shore.

Mākua Reef is one of the many long, wide fringing reefs on Kaua'i's north shore, and like the rest of these reefs, it is famous for throw-net fishing, a form of net fishing introduced by the first Japanese immigrants to Hawai'i and enthusiastically adopted by the Hawaiians. Throw-net fishermen are most commonly seen on low surf, low tide days when the reef emerges above sea level. They wait patiently along its outer edges for a school of fish to swim by and then throw their net over the school.

During periods of high surf, Tunnels turns into one of the

major surfing sites on Kaua'i. Waves that break on the west edge of Mākua Reef attract surfers from all over the island, and if the trade winds are strong enough, windsurfers arrive for surfing and wave jumping. Although high surf precludes all other water activities, it creates excellent beachcombing opportunities. Waves sweeping across Hā'ena Point deposit a great deal of debris on shore, including a wide variety of shells. Beachcombers are commonly seen walking the beach, scanning the debris line and sifting the sand for shells and other items of interest that have washed ashore.

All of these activities have made Tunnels an internationally famous beach, in constant use by visitors and residents.

# Lumaha'i Beach

**Location:** At the foot of Lumaha'i Valley along Highway 56. The beach is accessed from either its east end or west end. At the east end, beachgoers must park along the highway, then follow a trail down to the beach. At the west end, beachside parking is available in a grove of ironwood trees.

**Activities:** Bodyboarding, bodysurfing, swimming.

**Description:** Lumaha'i is approximately 4,000 feet long and varies from 200 to 400 feet in width, depending on the season. The foreshore is steep, and the ocean bottom drops abruptly to overhead depths. The entire beach is exposed to the open ocean with no fringing reef to protect it from high surf.

**Precautions:** During the winter months, high surf at Lumaha'i Beach creates a pounding shorebreak and powerful rip currents, making it one of the most dangerous beaches in Hawai'i. During one particularly tragic period from 1979 to 1988, ten people drowned here, all of them out-of-state visitors. Do not swim, body-surf, or bodyboard here if the surf is up. There are no lifeguards at this remote site, and there is no other rescue assistance nearby.

**Highlights:** Lumaha'i is one of the most scenic beaches in the Hawaiian Islands with its unspoiled setting of rugged volcanic mountains and lush greenery against a beautiful white sand beach and blue ocean. This panorama has been the inspiration for many paintings and the background for numerous advertisements, commercials, and movies, the best known of which is the now classic *South Pacific,* filmed in 1958. Most beachgoers gravitate to the east end of the beach, where a high lava point extends into the ocean forming a cove that offers some protection from the prevailing wind and the longshore currents. The beach is especially popular during the summer months, when the sand is at its widest and the surf is at its smallest.

Lumaha'i River, at the west end of the beach, is the only river left in Hawai'i that is untouched by development or diversion. Its nearly pristine waters form an estuary inland of the beach that supports native stream fish and shellfish and provides a habitat for several species of native stream birds. Lumaha'i Valley, now un-inhabited, was once an important agricultural area. It supported a succession of Hawaiian, Chinese, and finally Japanese farming communities that grew taro and later rice until the 1930s. At that time, rice production in California began to dominate the market, undercutting the price of Hawaiian rice and eventually leading to the demise of its production. Today, the valley is used only as a pasture for grazing cattle.

The meaning of *Lumaha'i* is unknown.

# Hanalei Bay

**Location:** Between Puʻupōā and Makahoa Points, Hanalei.

**Activities:** Boating, bodyboarding, bodysurfing, fishing, kayaking, outrigger canoe paddling, sailing, snorkeling, surfing, swimming, windsurfing.

**Description:** Hanalei Bay, the largest bay on Kauaʻi, is bordered by a white sand beach approximately two miles long and 125 feet wide. The beach is located between Hanalei River to the east and Waipā River to the west. Three rivers, Hanalei, Waiʻoli, and Waipā, cross the beach, mixing some stream-carried sediment into the beach sand at the east and west ends. Most of the beach, however, is clean, white sand. The ocean bottom slopes gently to overhead depths. Several shallow sandbars are located in the center of the beach. Large coral reefs are found only at the ends of the bay, Pu'u Pōā Reef to the east and Waikoko Reef to the west. Some smaller patch reefs are found in the center of the bay.

Three beach parks are located on Hanalei Bay: Black Pot Beach Park, Hanalei Pavilion Beach Park, and Wai'oli Beach Park. Each of them has restrooms, showers, and parking. Several public rights-of-way are also located along the bay. Black Pot Beach Park borders the mouth of the Hanalei River and is also the site of a public boat ramp and a 300-foot-long pier, the former Hanalei Landing.

**Precautions:** Hanalei Bay is subject to high surf, especially during the winter months. High surf generates a pounding shorebreak and powerful rip currents along the length of the beach that, over the years, have caused a number of drownings and near-drownings. Lifeguards are stationed at Black Pot Beach Park. Check with them before going in the water.

**Highlights:** *Hanalei* means "lei-shaped bay," a fitting description of this almost perfectly circular bay. With over two miles of clean, white sand bordering its inner margin and a backdrop of waterfalls and mountains peaks ranging from 1,000 to 4,000 feet high, Hanalei Bay is considered by many visitors and residents to be the most beautiful beach setting in Hawai'i. One of the best views of the beach is from the Princeville Hotel, located on the bluff above the east point of the bay.

In addition to its beauty, Hanalei Bay offers just about every ocean recreation activity in the islands, from boating to windsurfing. During periods of high surf, if you are not an expert bodyboarder or surfer, you can still kayak through the solitude of the taro fields along the Hanalei River.

Black Pot Beach Park, at the eastern corner of the bay, has for many years been the traditional gathering place for residents of Hanalei. The area was named after a large, black community cooking pot that sat in the park for many years, and although the pot is now long gone, residents still use the name and continue to congregate there. Hanalei Landing, the long pier at the west end of the park, was constructed in the early 1920s when interisland steamers were still the primary means of transportation. Today, the pier is used only for fishing and swimming. Off shore, the pier is a midbay anchorage on a sandy bottom at depths of thirty-five feet. Many yachts and other large boats anchor here during the calm summer months, when Hanalei Bay becomes a popular destination for trans-Pacific and interisland sailors.

# Secret Beach

**Location:** Between Kīlauea Point and Kalihiwai Bay, Kīlauea. A public right-of-way to the beach is located at the end of an unmarked dirt road that intersects Highway 56 just east of Kalihiwai Road. The right-of-way to the beach is a steep dirt trail.

**Activities:** Bodyboarding, bodysurfing, snorkeling, surfing, swimming.

**Description:** Secret Beach is a straight, flat white sand beach, approximately 3,000 feet long and 100 feet wide, that lies at the base of the sea cliffs west of Kīlauea Point. The backshore and sea cliffs are heavily vegetated with ironwood trees. The foreshore slopes gently to the water's edge. The ocean bottom fronting most of the beach is a series of shallow sandbars. Small trade wind-generated surf breaks constantly throughout the year on the sandbars, and high surf appears during the winter months. There are no facilities.

**Precautions:** High surf, especially during the winter months, generates a pounding shorebreak and powerful rip currents. There are no lifeguards at this remote beach.

**Highlights:** Secret Beach is not visible from Kūhiō Highway or from any of the other roads above it. From land, it can only be seen from Kīlauea Point National Wildlife Refuge to the east. For this reason, its location for many years was known only to area residents, and its name was Kauapea Beach. In the 1970s it was "discovered" during the national hippie movement which brought many young mainlanders to Hawai'i. Having rejected the social values of their parents, they were experimenting with alternate lifestyles and were especially advocating a return to the land and to simple, subsistence living. Secret Beach became one of their transient camps. Today, the hippies are long gone, but the name they gave the beach still remains.

Secret Beach offers spectacular scenery, with clean, white sand, a backdrop of green sea cliffs, Kīlauea Lighthouse, and Moku-'ae'ae Island off shore. Ocean conditions are often dangerous during the winter, but it is a popular swimming site during the summer when the ocean is calmer. Its isolated splendor has also made it one of the most popular nudist beaches in Hawai'i. Nude sunbathing is not legal, but it is common on many remote beaches.

# Ocean Recreation Activities

## Bodyboarding and Bodysurfing

Bodyboarding and bodysurfing are wave-riding sports that are often practiced in close proximity. Bodysurfers use only their bodies to ride a wave, whereas bodyboarders lie prone on a small foam bodyboard that supports their upper bodies. Riders in both sports wear fins for added propulsion. Bodyboarding and bodysurfing are popular because the required equipment is inexpensive and easy to transport. Fins and bodyboards may be purchased at sporting goods stores or surf shops or rented at beach concessions.

## Kayaking

Kayaking has two common forms in Hawai'i: ocean racing and ocean touring. Ocean racing appeals to competitive paddlers who enjoy the challenge of racing in the open ocean. Their boat of choice is the surf ski, a narrow, twenty-foot-long kayak, with its bow upturned like a water ski. Developed in Australia for competition in the ocean, surf skis are designed primarily for straight ahead speed. Ocean touring, on the other hand, is a leisurely form of kayaking and provides opportunities for paddlers to explore Hawai'i's shorelines, bays, and small offshore islets. In contrast to surf skis, ocean touring kayaks are wide and stable. They range from nine to sixteen feet in length, and they are easy to carry, launch, and land. Ocean kayak rentals and tours are available on all the major islands.

## Sailing

One of the most popular sailing crafts in Hawai'i is the catamaran, a twin-hulled sailboat that was patterned after the ancient Polynesian double-hull sailing canoes. Beach catamarans are small, light-weight boats that range from fourteen to twenty-one feet long. Novices may attempt catamaran sailing, but it is a skill that should be learned from an experienced sailor. Lessons and rentals can be arranged from beach concessions on all the major islands.

## Snorkeling and Scuba Diving

The nearshore waters that surround the Hawaiian Islands contain diverse marine life and spectacular underwater terrain. Some of the world's best snorkeling and scuba diving sites are found here. Island waters are warm throughout the year, and most snorkelers are comfortable wearing only a swim suit. Scuba divers are adequately protected by only a wetsuit jacket. Novice snorkelers and scuba divers can arrange for lessons and equipment rentals through beach concessions, tour desks, and dive shops.

## Surfing

Hawai'i has some of the best surfing sites in the world, from small beginners' breaks on the south shores to for-experts-only breaks on the north shores. Surfers unfamiliar with the islands should check at lifeguard towers, beach concessions, and surf shops for advice on equipment and local wave conditions. Novice surfers should go to Waikīkī and take a lesson before heading off on their own. Anyone visiting O'ahu during the winter months should include a visit to the North Shore, the mecca of big wave surfing, for a first-hand look at some of the world's best surfers in action.

## Swimming

Swimming is the most popular water activity in Hawai'i, and good swimming opportunities are found at almost all of Hawai'i's beaches, especially during periods of little or no surf. All of Hawai'i's best beaches are sand beaches, where walking in and out of the water with bare feet is comfortable.

## Windsurfing

Windsurfing was introduced to Hawai'i in the early 1970s and is well established on all the major islands. The Hawaiian Islands, with their warm waters, year-round trade winds, and challenging surf, provide some of the best windsurfing locations in the world. The most heavily windsurfed area in Hawai'i today is the shoreline of Maui between Kahului and Ho'okipa. Beach concessions and windsurfing shops on all the major islands offer lessons and equipment rentals.

# Water Safety

## Marine Injuries

None of Hawai'i's reef animals are normally aggressive toward people, but some of them have pincers, teeth, or poisonous stingers, and others are covered with spines, thorns or bristles. Chance encounters with these animals may lead to injuries. The best book on the subject is *All Stings Considered: First Aid and Medical Treatment of Hawai'i's Marine Injuries* by Craig Thomas and Susan Scott (University of Hawai'i Press, 1997). The following sections include the most common marine injuries, and a few words about sharks and sunburn.

## Coral Cuts

Corals and coralline algae are the most common reef builders in Hawai'i. Contacts with these reefs account for most of the scratches and cuts suffered by swimmers, snorkelers, divers, and surfers. These cuts are susceptible to infection and may be slow to heal. Contrary to popular belief, coral lodged in a cut will not continue to grow, but it should be removed because of the high risk of infection. Clean cuts thoroughly with soap, water, and hydrogen peroxide, and apply an antiseptic as soon as possible. Severe cuts may need to be stitched by a physician.

## Portuguese Man-of-War Stings

The Portuguese man-of-war is a marine jellyfish that drifts on the surface of the ocean. To control its drift, it inflates and deflates its most recognizable body part, a small, crested blue bubble, approximately two inches long. The man-of-war trolls for food by trailing a long tentacle under the bubble. The tentacle is covered with nematocysts, or stinging cells, and these minute venom-filled cells paralyze tiny fish or other prey that the man-of-war transports to its mouth by retracting the tentacle.

During periods of strong onshore winds, Portuguese man-of-war are commonly blown ashore, where they encounter swimmers, surfers, and anyone else in the ocean. A tentacle needs only to brush the skin to cause a burning sensation, and if it wraps around a body part, such as the neck, an arm, or a leg, it will deliver a painful sting. Tentacle sections that have wrapped around a body part should be washed off immediately with saltwater or fresh water.

Man-of-war stings may leave visible marks on the skin, such as blisters or welts, but the pain will usually subside within thirty minutes. Man-of-war stings, however, like those of bees and other insects, can cause severe reactions in people who are allergic to venom. If any unusual symptoms occur, take the victim to an emergency room immediately.

## Box Jellyfish Stings

Box jellyfish, like their brethren the Portuguese man-of-war, are small marine jellyfish from one to three inches long. They get their name from their transparent, box-shaped bells and troll for food by trailing four pink-tinted tentacles, one from each of the bell's four corners. Box jellyfish feed on small fish and shrimp, stinging them with the nematocysts on their tentacles. Unlike the man-of-war, however, they are not surface-bound and can swim slowly in any direction, including up and down.

Hawai'i's box jellyfish seem to appear on a monthly cycle. They invade nearshore waters about seven to ten days after the full moon. The most dangerous time for stings seems to be from daybreak to mid-morning, when the jellyfish are near the surface. As the sun rises, the light-sensitive creatures settle down to deeper waters and only return to the surface after dark. They stay for about three days, then disappear until the next full moon.

Box jellyfish tentacles brushing the skin or wrapping around a body part will deliver an immediate, painful, burning sting. Tentacle sections that have wrapped around a body part should be washed off immediately with salt or fresh water. The stings may leave visible marks on the skin, such as blisters or welts, but the pain will usually subside within thirty minutes. Box jellyfish stings, however, like those of bees and other insects, can cause severe reactions in people who are allergic to venom. If any unusual symptoms occur, take the victim to an emergency room immediately.

## Sea Urchin Punctures

Sea urchins, commonly known by their Hawaiian name, *wana,* are covered with sharp, brittle, needlelike spines. The spines easily puncture skin and usually break off with the slightest contact. Small embedded spine fragments may be left in the skin, where they will naturally extrude or dissolve, but larger fragments may have to be removed manually, sometimes by a doctor, if they are especially deep. Punctures cause an immediate, intense, burning pain which may last for an hour or more. If any unusual symptoms occur after the initial pain, take the victim to an emergency room immediately.

## Shark Attacks

Sharks are common in Hawaiian waters but usually do not pose a threat to swimmers. If you meet a shark face-to-face, the following are some actions you might take. Retreat and swim to safety, especially if the shark is a tiger or a great white. These two types of sharks have been implicated in most of the shark attacks in Hawai‘i. Do not make any erratic or thrashing motions that might be interpreted as signs of panic. If you are injured and bleeding, get out of the water as soon as possible. And finally, do not swim in murky or muddy waters, especially where rivers or streams empty into the ocean after heavy rains. Sharks are scavengers and commonly patrol these murky areas, especially at dawn and dusk.

## Sunburn

Sunburn is skin damage that is caused by overexposure to the ultraviolet rays of the sun. When human skin is subjected to ultraviolet radiation, it increases its production of melanin, the brown pigment in skin cells, and this protective response is known as tanning, the goal of sunbathing. However, when skin is overexposed to the sun, the ultraviolet rays burn the underlying blood vessels and damage cells, resulting in sunburn. Long-term effects of regular sunburn may include premature aging and skin cancer.

Sunburn can happen to anyone, but people with light colored skin are especially susceptible. To reduce severe incidents of sunburn, avoid prolonged sun exposures between mid-morning and mid-afternoon, when ultraviolet rays are most intense, and use a lotion with a sun-protection factor (SPF) of 30 or higher at all times. Remember that ultraviolet rays reflect off of sand, water, and concrete, so being under a beach umbrella or a shady tree is not a substitute for SPF lotion. Consider going to the beach early in the morning or later in the afternoon. You will avoid not only the harshest ultraviolet rays but the largest crowds on the beach.

## Dangerous Water Conditions

Many of Hawai'i's best beaches are not protected by reefs, points of land, or other natural barriers. This lack of protection allows high surf to come directly ashore, where it generates strong currents and other dangerous water conditions. Visitors who are not familiar with the ocean need to be aware that they may encounter pounding shorebreaks and fast-flowing rip currents, conditions which may endanger the lives of even the strongest swimmers. Although many of Hawai'i's beaches are staffed by lifeguards, just as many are not. If you arrive at an unguarded beach and are not sure if conditions are dangerous, ask a local resident. If no one else is around, err on the side of safety and do not go in the water.

## Rip Currents

Rip currents are fast-flowing, riverlike movements of water that travel seaward from shallow, nearshore areas. They are generated by surf and are found wherever waves are breaking, whether on a reef or on a sandbar. Sets of incoming waves bring large volumes of water into nearshore areas, and as the water accumulates near the beach, it begins to flow along shore or back out through the surf, forming a rip current. As the current picks up speed, it will tow an unsuspecting swimmer seaward into the open ocean.

Rip currents can be seen from the beach as they travel seaward. They flatten incoming waves, and at sandy beaches they resemble small, foamy rivers as they carry sand and other suspended debris. Rip currents are short-lived and die out at the surf line, usually within 100 yards of the beach. If you are caught in one, ride with it until it loses its power and then swim back to the beach on either side of it. If you are too tired to swim ashore, float beyond the surf line and wait for help. Near-drowning situations occur when swimmers panic and fight the current by swimming against it, tiring themselves to the point of complete exhaustion.

Many swimmers use the words "undertow" and "rip current" interchangeably, but rip currents do not pull swimmers underwater as the word undertow implies. The undertow phenomenon only occurs when a rip current flows into breaking waves. The rip will continue to move seaward, and a swimmer caught in the current will feel as if he is being towed under water as waves break over him.

## Shorebreaks

Shorebreaks are nearshore surf zones where waves break close to or directly on a beach. Shorebreak waves from one to two feet high generally pose little threat to wave riders and provide good bodysurfing and bodyboarding opportunities, but waves three feet or higher can generate dangerous water conditions. As waves increase in size, they break with considerable downward force, often slamming inexperienced swimmers into the shallow ocean bottom and causing loss of breath, disorientation, or injury. Anyone even temporarily incapacitated in the surf is a potential drowning candidate. As a general rule, waves that are waist high or higher should be considered dangerous. Keep in mind that the majority of drownings, near-drownings, rescues, and beach injuries in Hawai'i occur at shorebreak sites.

Visitors should be aware that drowning victims have included not only shorebreak swimmers but sightseers who have ventured too close to high surf sweeping across a beach or a rocky ledge overlooking the ocean. These individuals have been knocked off their feet by unexpectedly large waves and hauled into the powerful turmoil of high surf, where they have drowned. If you are in a high surf area, keep well away from wet sand and wet rocks, the places where waves are washing.

# Index

# About the Author

**John R. Kukeakalani Clark,** born and raised in Hawai'i, is Deputy Fire Chief of the Honolulu Fire Department. In his popular book series—*The Beaches of O'ahu, The Beaches of Maui County, Beaches of the Big Island,* and *Beaches of Kaua'i and Ni'ihau*—Clark shares his extensive knowledge and deep respect for Hawai'i's shoreline, his concern for the safety of beachgoing residents and visitors, and his commitment to protect and preserve Hawaiian culture, place names, and legends.